Hack the Mobile Lifestyle

6 Steps to Work Well and Play More!

By Marcey Rader, M.Ed., CPFT, CPES

This book is dedicated to Summer Busto, my first mobile professional.

Acknowledgements

A super-duper huge THANK YOU to my husband Kevin for supporting me in breaking free of the golden handcuffs so I could march to the beat of my OWN drummer! Thank you to Lish Marker for editing in exchange for a Sprigs Wrist Banjee. Thank you to Kyle Held for being one of my first clients, my marketing mastermind and for not letting me get sucked in to playing it safe and sacrificing my personality. Thank you to Melissa Gheen for being one of the best business buddies a start-up gal could ask for. Thank you to my business coach Megan J. Huber for putting me on the right path to make my business successful and coming up with the title, which was harder than writing the book! Thank you to the San Diego SMIT class of 2013 that inspired me (unknowingly) to leave my job and do this full time. Thank you to Jackie Cunning for supporting me in my work hacking techniques and encouraging me to train others. Lastly, thank you to all the flight attendants, pilots, hotel staff, car rental attendants, and baristas who made a mobile life a little easier to handle.

Table of Contents

Welcome

Hello Mobile Professional, Road Warrior, or Traveler!

Have you ever walked up and down an airplane terminal trying to find a healthy meal or worked out in an overheated, humid hotel room with only two pieces of working equipment?

Have you ever felt like your Inbox controlled you and you had no idea how to keep up with your travel calendar and tasks while on the road?

You bought this book because you either

a) Just got a job as a mobile professional and don't want to end up looking like the other people you work with (haggard, tired and older than they are).

b) Are currently a mobile professional and want to *stop* looking haggard, tired and older than you are!

You made the right purchase. Other books can tell you how to be fit or they can tell you how to be productive but as a mobile professional for ten years, I know first hand how difficult it is to stay healthy and productive while traveling. Really, how can a person be productive if they aren't healthy and how can they be healthy without being productive? A job that requires travel isn't just a job. It's a lifestyle. Until someone has worked a nine-hour day, rushed to the airport, sat on the tarmac for an hour, didn't have time to get dinner in between flights and subsisted on nothing but a 45-calorie bag of pretzels until they checked in to their hotel where the restaurant was closed and the options were beef jerky and Nutri-grain bars....whew! Well then, they haven't traveled for business!

The 6 Steps to Work Well and Play More System is a comprehensive guide that covers exercise, nutrition and productivity in the areas of:

1. Air Travel
2. Hotel
3. Auto and Train
4. Mobile Office
5. Restaurants, parties and meetings
6. Home

By the end of this book you will have learned ways to:

- Maintain your health and actually *improve* it.

- Be productive digitally and physically.

- Pack lean but mean (I *mean* business and I am going to exercise!)

- Maintain relationships.

- Keep your house from falling apart.

I'm not going to pretend that all of this will be easy. My favorite quote is *'Talk doesn't cook rice'*. You can talk about cooking rice all day but unless you boil the water and throw in the rice, you are going to go hungry my friend. Join me in this journey to make small behavior changes that will result in a significant impact on your travel and personal life.

Who is Marcey Rader?

I have tried and failed and tried and succeeded at different things on my path to personal growth, health, and productivity. I'm going to share them with you, no holds barred. I have raced in endurance and ultra-endurance events since 2000 and have managed to improve my diet every year of my adult life. I figured out a routine at home with my husband that, even though it doesn't work perfectly, opens the door to more cooperation for both of us. I have also had a date with my husband every week (unless I was traveling for more than seven days straight) for twenty years. I took a graduate course online during a heavy semester of travel and have taken other courses or performed in depth research to grow personally and make major life changes.

My job as a corporate trainer was to teach systems, tools and procedures but my favorite thing to teach were modules on Travel Health and Work Hacking that I developed out of personal interest. They always received the best feedback out of the entire three-week course. My boss was so impressed by what I was able to achieve personally with my work hacks, I was asked to teach an informal course to my training team which became part of our annual developmental goals. I had been a Personal Trainer on the side for twenty years and loved teaching people how to be healthy. This was when I realized my passion was in teaching people how to be productive and healthy. I realized the people who needed it most were the people I was dealing with every day: Mobile Professionals.

My own accomplishments, while leading a life of business travel include:

- 12+ marathons

- 30+ triathlons sprint to Iron distance

- 20+ adventure races of 6-30 hours in length (including 2 National Championships races)

- 4 ultra running races

- 10+ mountain bike races 6-12 hours

- Hiking the Grand Canyon Rim to Rim to Rim

- Decluttering my home and then downsizing to live in one of my dream locations next to a state park.

- Shutting down my email every day with no more than 10 emails in my inbox for over four years (and most of the time – zero!)

- Staying debt free except for my house.

- Maintaining my personal growth exploration with one habit at a time for the last five years.

Testimonials

"Marcey has given me three simple life-altering things I'm supposed to do when I wake up in the mornings. When I do them I never fail to have a great day. When I don't, it's shit"

K. Held, Marketing Director, Mobile Professional

"I started working with Marcey a little over a year ago and I hired her to help me understand what I needed to do to get my workouts back on track. She took the time to learn my needs both personally and professionally and outlined a program that was easy for me to follow and balanced those needs. She helped me to understand what I needed to do to be effective and productive in order to reach my goals in a very efficient way. I really enjoyed working with Marcey. She was my biggest cheerleader. She made herself available and made all the tools I needed extremely easy and accessible. I highly recommend Marcey if you are looking for someone who understands complex problems and you want to be more efficient in your personal and professional life."

S. Busto, Associate Director, Human Resources, Mobile Professional

"Marcey has done an outstanding job of addressing virtually every issue that travelers face when it comes to accomplishing their work and enjoying their life if it involves travel! It's a book every traveler should keep handy, because you're sure to find new tips and techniques every time you pick it up. It's fun to read and there are many suggestions you can begin implementing immediately."

B. Hemphill, The Productive Environment Institute

5

"I HIGHLY recommend this book. Anyone with a mobile job, whether in airports or on the road, knows it is difficult to stay healthy and organized. I have already implemented 2-3 EASY habits and have reduced stress and remained so much more organized! The tips and tricks are easily transferable to a variety of lifestyles. This is an easy read, jam-packed with valuable advice from someone who's been there!"

-R. Armstrong

"This is one amazing read, whether you're a mobile professional or not! Marcey is truly an expert and is gifted at going into depth while keeping you hooked. I can feel her energy and enthusiasm bursting off the pages. Never ever would I have thought that a book about productivity, health and travel could be so engaging, uplifting, funny and kick-ass. She really put her heart into it and the information she researched is impressive."

-E. Schultz, The Technicolor Priestess

"Having more than 1000 emails in my inbox and sent folder is stressful. I used to worry about things I was sure I'd missed and would rely on people to contact me again for urgent issues that I hadn't addressed. I usually felt overwhelmed with work. Marcey gave me some tips on how to clean out my in/sent folders only handling emails once - deleting or filing them as soon as I addressed them. To start, I blocked off some time over a few days and went through my email to clean it out. My goal was to have no more than 10 emails still there at the end of each day. It took some discipline and the techniques I learned from Marcey but it quickly became a habit. Now I easily see what is urgent and can take care of it as required. My stress levels have significantly decreased and I don't feel as busy or overwhelmed every day."

J. Cunning, Associate Director

The Struggle Story

Getting to this point wasn't kittens and rainbows or cake and ice cream. I definitely struggled. I became interested in exercise when I was 18 and decided I didn't want to be chubby anymore. I was also interested in nutrition but what I thought was healthy eating wasn't actually healthy at all. That may be the hardest thing to swallow, no pun intended. What I thought I was doing was a good thing but found out from ever-evolving research and experience that actually, it wasn't! When you eat a bacon double cheeseburger you know it isn't the best choice. When I was eating frozen yogurt instead of ice cream or a soy burger instead of a hamburger I thought I was doing the right thing. Boy was I wrong. It wasn't just ignorance though, nutrition knowledge and research has grown exponentially in the last decade.

When I started traveling for business I was a vegetarian. A bad vegetarian. I didn't eat nearly enough vegetables and did what a lot of new vegetarians do, which is eat meat analogues. What the heck is an analogue? They are fake meat products like soy burgers, fake chicken, fake sausage, etc. For some people I still think this is a good way to wean off of meat products but ONLY if they don't expect it to taste like meat. It cracks me up when I am eating a veggie burger or a mock 'something or other' and someone asks me "but does it taste like chicken"? "No, because it isn't chicken!" Does apple pie taste like lasagna? No, because it's apple pie! It's still very convenient though when you are at a BBQ or want a quick fix. It's kind of like deli meat sandwiches. They aren't good for you but eating them only occasionally out of convenience is not going to *kill* you (although the sodium, nitrates and nitrites in deli meat are REALLY bad for you. Don't do it.)

Anyway, because airports had very few vegetarian options, if any, I subsisted on frozen yogurt and soft pretzels for a good part of the early 2000s. I thought eating this way was at least better than eating meat. WRONG. I was eating processed, refined carbohydrates and sugars. I also became addicted to Frappucinos as a treat. Because I got it without whip, how bad could it be? *Bad.* Very bad and still super high in sugar. Artificial sweeteners were also big in my diet. Sugar-free this and low-sugar that. Now that I know how bad artificial sweeteners are and how the 'healthfulness' of it is one of the worst nutritional conspiracies in the history of history, I weaned myself off of those as well.

It was also hard, and sometimes still is, to have my meals picked for me, for example, at business meetings or conferences where I have no control. Ten years ago, most people didn't even consider vegetarians when they were planning a menu. I also didn't like to call attention to my diet in those circumstances and would sometimes end up eating things I didn't really want to and feel bad about it later.

When I traveled internationally I sometimes found it hard because of the time of day people would eat. I am an early dinner eater and so when I used to go to Argentina, I would wander around trying to find something besides an empanada before 8pm. It was a window of about 4 hours where if I didn't get a meal by 4pm, I wasn't going to get another one until after 8pm and I didn't like eating that late. I also had a hard time because not all countries put the ingredients or nutritional information on their labels. I am a label looker so I would get a little anxiety about what I was eating (or not eating). I remember learning after three months in London drinking hot chocolate all the time that it was so good because they used whole milk and Cadbury's! I am adventurous though, and like to eat the local food wherever I am. When my brother and I were in Beijing we just ate what was put in front of us. Sometimes, it's just best not to ask.

I was completely addicted to sugar. I would eat protein bars (sugar), drink Frappucinos (sugar), and get a dessert like a cookie or brownie to take home and share with my husband...sugar sugar sugar. I had to have a sweet treat every night. I was always really fit but never really lean until I started eating lots more vegetables and way way *way* less sugar. I was never able to see my abs until I changed my diet and cut out sugar, artificial sweeteners and added a serious amount of vegetables. Abs are made in the kitchen.

My struggles with productivity were mostly internal. I have always been fast at typing, reading and 'doing' of whatever task I was performing, but am very easily distracted and still have to work on it. I would get anxious if I couldn't check my email often enough. I had so many RSS feeds of items I wanted to read I always felt behind. One year, I cashed in my ready-to-expire Delta points for magazines. This was a big mistake because I got behind in reading those too. It made me feel like I had much less time than I did because I had so much to read it seemed like a part-time job.

My last corporate job had me on the phone up to six hours a day in meetings. How companies think you can get anything done with that kind of schedule is beyond me, but that was my life. Thankfully, I have always worked from home when I wasn't traveling so I could at least throw a load of laundry in while listening to 50 minutes of a 60-minute call that wasn't at all relevant to me.

I've never tried to keep up with the Joneses much but I started getting into expensive sports like triathlon and adventure racing. At one point, I had four bikes. I rode them all, but still...how many people need four bikes? I had books and CDs I didn't read or listen to and clothes I didn't wear. I also lived in a house with a yard that I hated landscaping and my husband hated mowing. It caused friction between us and wasn't worth it. Who wants to argue about yard work?

And then there is the question of who does what chores. Me, because I'm gone all week and need to contribute to the house or my husband who is home all week and is the one there most of the time messing it up?

What changed? I read the book The Power of Less by Leo Babauta and my life path was forever altered. I decided to make small changes based on topics from the book. I also started reading every minimalist and decluttering blog I could find, got hooked on productivity websites and started looking at myself from a different point of view. The **difficult** point of view. I made a one-year plan on an Excel spreadsheet and put the current behavior change on a whiteboard in my home office/exercise studio. I decided on changing one habit at a time in productivity and one habit at a time in my health or personal growth. I also picked one room or area in the house to declutter. I did each habit/room for 6-8 weeks, depending on how hard it was to change, and put a little check on my whiteboard every day that I did it. Now there are great apps that can help you keep track of habit changes, like Lift.do, but back then, there was just my whiteboard. Some things were very easy (adding more fruit!) and others were not (checking email less often) but after two years I had made it through all of the habits I wanted to change or create as well as every room in my house. Was I finished? No way! I will never finish growing and becoming better but I don't have or need as detailed a game plan as before.

Some of my habit changes, which I will also touch on in the book, were:

- Checking email 4 x per day

- The Pomodoro Technique

- Writing and responding to most emails in five sentences or less

- Turning off Instant Message

- Not checking email or working on the computer at least an hour before bed

- Increasing my fruit intake

- Increasing my vegetable intake

- Decreasing my sugar intake

- Eliminating artificial sweeteners

- Decreasing processed food intake

- Planning appropriately for work-related meals (much easier now with all the apps and websites)

- Decluttering every room in my house

- Decluttering my closet until I only had what fits and makes me feel confident

- Downsizing my home

- Saving enough money to pay cash for a new car

- Decreasing my intake of advertisements and news

I'm sure I'm forgetting some things but these were the main ones.

Myths

It is a myth that mobile professionals are always stressed, fat, unhealthy and chronically tired. There are many studies that say business travel is stressful but there are also studies that say it can be less stressful because we don't have to deal with home stressors e.g. errands, chores, and demands of our family members. I would agree that it is both. I can certainly say that it doesn't have to be stressful and a lot of the stress that you do feel is triggered by your response to things that are out of your control (like plane delays) or lack of planning (like not buying snacks for the plane) or just plain not taking care of yourself. You might feel like eating healthy is impossible but with proper planning you can do it *most* of the time. I'm not going to lie and say you can do it 100% of the time because it would be unrealistic given some of the dismal choices in airports. Your exercise situation may not be *perfect* but you can adapt and find something to do to keep your energy and strength up and your stress and weight down.

As far as productivity – most people don't actually expect you to respond immediately to email and our need to check it is brought about by our own anxiety. Flight delay? Out of your control. Make use of your time and do something else like walking around the airport, following up on a call or reading that post you've had bookmarked for two weeks, rather than stress about it. Where the anger flows….the energy goes.

This book is going to go through several habits related to business travel and how to be more productive and healthy. You may not need all of the solutions so feel free to jump around. Before we get into anything specific, I want to outline how I managed to make behavior changes and how it might help you too. It might not seem relevant but I think the examples are important to see that they don't all happen at once and change can be made a little piece at a time.

Behaviour Change

I would consider myself disciplined, methodical and systematic. I have had at least four different people, upon describing me, put their hands in a position like they are holding a box and say, "You are very"…and then move their hands three times to the right. In my head I would think they were saying 'You are very ordered, strict, neat, disciplined, rigid'. I didn't really know and it used to bother me until my orthopedist, Dr. Rob Jones, upon doing it, said "Systematic. You understand there is a process and you follow that process in a certain order". I'll take that. I like to say that those three movements people make when they describe me stands for "Gets Shit Done".

When I first started my massive self-improvement plan I was very realistic and planned well (back to that methodical, systematic, ordered mentality). The first thing I did was started writing behaviors, habits or projects down in Evernote and would add to them as I thought of more. After about a month, I went through them and ordered them by importance, dividing them into two categories – Easy and Hard. I didn't want to do 2-3 hard changes at once since I was working on three different areas: Physical clutter, Electronic Organization and Mind/Body. I wish I had kept the list of all the changes but I no longer have that list and am going by memory alone. I'll go through my top three and what I did for each one.

I put three columns on my whiteboard – Mind/Body, Electronic, and Physical. Then I put a behavior change or project under each one and gave myself 6-8 weeks to accomplish the goal or change. I started with the easy ones for the first month.

Mind/Body

Eat more fruit. This one was actually pretty easy but I didn't eat fruit every day and wanted to put more in my diet. I didn't eat a ton of vegetables so I thought I would just start with fruit. Week One – Eat one serving of fruit every day. Each day I did this I put an X next to it. Week Two – Eat two servings of fruit daily. Week Three – Eat three servings of fruit daily. I continued this for six weeks. I made sure I got a minimum of three but didn't keep increasing past three. If I ate more than that, fine, but if not, that was okay because I needed to work on the second step, which was much harder.

Eat more vegetables. I continued with the same path as before except this time, I went up to five servings a day. I used one serving for Week 1, two servings for Weeks 2-3, three servings for Weeks 4-5, four servings for Weeks 6-7 and five servings for Week 8. I believe I had to stretch this out another four weeks but I eventually got it and I eat a serious amount of vegetables daily now. I usually have no trouble getting in 5-11 servings a day of fruits and vegetables. One thing that helped was I joined an incredible Community Supported Agriculture program, Papa Spuds, where I can pick my food and they deliver to my door once a week. They categorize offerings according to local/non-local, conventional/organic/pesticide free and feature more than plant foods. They sell meats, fish, breads/grains, sauces, dairy, eggs, spices, and coffee. I have referred several people to them and I can say that this little business has changed my life and my husband's. I LOVE vegetables now and regularly eat things that growing up, I didn't even know existed.

My family doesn't eat a lot of vegetables so I wasn't exposed to many until adulthood. I grew up eating corn, potatoes and green beans as the only vegetables that were served, which is funny, because I don't even consider the first two vegetables anymore – just starches, and green beans are legumes! I had never had a pepper, beet, cucumber, kale, or squash until I was at least in my late-twenties. Now they are staples. One year when we got home from a week with my family at Christmas, I steamed an entire bag of broccoli, sprinkled nutritional yeast on it and sat down and ate it. I'm not talking about the single serving bags either – the *family size* bag! I craved veggies that much. I would also consider myself a cabbaholic or kalaholic. I eat cabbage and kale like some people eat chips. I can eat a whole bag of it and have to actually pace myself sometimes. Yep, the girl who hadn't tried kale until she was 35 years old.

Eat less sugar. Ok, so you know how I didn't eat fruits and vegetables growing up? Replace that with sugar. That's what I ate. My family members are major sugarholics except for my brother. He eats sugar but not as much as the rest of us. My husband also comes from a family of sugarholics. We had a serious habit of needing a treat after dinner each night. I also drank a hot chocolate or mocha latte almost daily when I traveled, and was on a mission to make sure I showed up at every site visit with a Frappuccino or mocha latte. I would also buy the giant cookies or some other kind of dessert and fly home with it to share with my husband. I ate a lot of added sugar in the form of granola bars and protein bars, and drank a lot of drinks like Crystal Light.

The first thing I started doing was asking for less mocha in my lattes. Do you know that in a Grande/medium they put four pumps of syrup??? Sometimes six! I started with half the pumps, and then went down to one pump and now half a pump. At home I put 1-2 tablespoons of almond milk and a tablespoon of 100% pure unsweetened cocoa powder and that does it for me. No sugar! When I think about it, I'll go ahead and put my cocoa powder in my reusable cup if I'm going to a local coffee date. So much better for me. I also started drinking a lot more tea and can now easily drink tea with no sugar. It wasn't until this year that I learned that tea is high in pesticides and it is really important to buy organic. It's also better to buy loose since the bags they put them in sometimes have plastics that just disintegrate in your cup. Yum….plastic tea!

As for the desserts, I started with buying the cookie and immediately throwing half of it away. Then I was sharing a quarter of it with my husband until I stopped buying them altogether. I was using meal per diem so I didn't care about the wasted money. One day I took everything in my cabinets and fridge and weighed the grams of sugar on a scale. Once you put that powdery white stuff in a dish and see how much sugar you are ACTUALLY eating it is astounding. One packet of sugar is four grams. Twelve grams of sugar is a tablespoon. My Grande Frappuccino light that I favored had over two tablespoons of sugar. My nonfat Grande mocha latte had three tablespoons. I used to love Starbucks flavored Vias for the convenience until I realized they have a tablespoon too! A travel convenience that I used, Zone Perfect bars, have over a tablespoon per bar. If you want to cut down on your sugar intake, measure out your sugar. When you realize there are three packets of sugar in that one little bar it may make you think twice.

Does this mean I eat no sugar? No. I still like it but I definitely don't crave it like in the past and can easily say no. I decided a couple of years ago to set a food rule to only eat sweets on the weekends unless it is a holiday or our monthaversary (our first date was Ben and Jerry's and we have gone to Ben and Jerry's the 19th of every month for twenty years!). I have managed to go through three weeks of corporate training where desserts are offered daily and not have a sweet once because for me, it may be a slippery slope. Now that my tastes have changed, I sometimes go the whole weekend and on Monday realize 'I forgot to have a treat!' because I'm just not thinking about them.

Other nutritional habits I changed: No artificial sweeteners (including sucralose) except for chewing gum for about 2 minutes if it is offered to me (they must be hinting that my breath smells like road kill) and less meat analogues (only occasionally and the least processed as possible).

Electronic

Turn Instant Message off. The company I worked for installed Microsoft Communicator on our machines and at first I thought it was great. I could IM my colleagues all day, get quick answers, ask questions during a call…it was fun! Then I started realizing how much it interfered with what I was doing. As I started researching productivity the message was clear; instant message, pop-up notifications and even having a 'new mail' envelope icon is bad for your productivity. I made a new rule for myself and the ultimate goal was to only have it on when I was doing menial tasks like loading things into our learning management system (sloooooowwwww), my timesheet, expense reports, etc. and I definitely had it off the first and last hour that I worked every day. This one was actually pretty easy which is why it was my first habit change. I also used the 'appear offline' function and made sure that I wasn't automatically signed in when I started the computer.

Check Email Less. This was much harder. I got serious anxiety by not checking email often because I felt guilty or that I would miss something. I was afraid my boss would know or someone would need me and I wouldn't be available right away. I started putting it into perspective. If I was traveling, people weren't able to reach me and the world didn't end. When I was conducting a training class people were unable to reach me for 3-4 hours at a time and the sun still rose and set. I downloaded a program called Rescue Time which showed my productivity online by the week, day and how much time I spent in different applications. What an eye opener! My job description should have just said 1) Read email. 2) Respond to email. I was spending way too much time in email. To wean myself and not have a full-on anxiety attack, I started working offline more. I would download all my emails in the morning and then work offline for one hour. Every hour I would go back online and send/receive and then do it again for another hour. I found very quickly that I was able to get so much more done and no one seemed to notice. I started extending my time until I was just checking four times per day. I should mention I started first with my personal email and then moved to my work email. It was a full six months before I told my boss I only sent/received four times a day. She had never noticed and as a matter of fact, was so impressed she wanted me to teach others what I had learned. By doing this, I was able to take my inbox to zero and for four years, have had no more than 10 emails in my inbox a handful of times and most of the time, I have zero. I try to only check my personal account twice daily and my work account four times daily. Currently, I am trying out email free Sundays and eventually want to move to email free weekends.

This habit is often the first to go when I am traveling. Not so much out of anxiety as out of ease of use. I have an iPhone so if I am sitting on the tarmac, waiting in line etc., I can easily check. I try to catch up on blogs and news instead but occasionally I will have to have an intervention with myself.

Reduce RSS feeds. I love to read and I love to learn. When I first started subscribing to RSS feeds I subscribed to everything I was interested in and stayed subscribed. I used to be one of those people who had to finish a book or movie even if it was meh (finish what you started mentality). I was so excited about learning productivity, minimalism and organization techniques and research I would read one blog and if they mentioned another blog, I would read that one too. It was mentally exhausting. One day I decided I was going to max out at five (I do this with podcasts too) and have stayed that way since. I also decided that if I were more than five posts behind on one feed, I would mark 'all as read'. I turned off the badge notification so I wouldn't see how many posts that were new, taunting me about how far behind I was. If I found that a couple of sites were similar or cross-posted a lot, I got rid of the least favorite or relevant to me. I also stopped giving myself a hard time about the feeds that had several posts per day. There is no way I could keep up and it wasn't important for me to either. The only person that was saying it was important was me! My husband is addicted to Reddit so if there is some current event or meme I must know about I count on him to give me the scoop.

Other things I did. Reduced the size of my emails and try to subscribed to the Five Sentences or less philosophy, stopped writing the 'thanks' emails that just clutter people's inboxes, used more meaningful subject lines, and worked in batches using the Pomodoro Technique (more on that later).

Physical

Clothes. I used to love clothes and loved shopping. I have seriously whittled down my closet in the last four years and I think most people would be surprised just how few clothes I have. I love it. It makes getting ready so much easier because I don't have as many things to choose from. It also makes me really consider when I am making a purchase. The first thing I did was get rid of the obvious things that didn't fit me well or I was just 'meh' about. I asked myself the following questions:

1) If I saw this in a store today, would I purchase it?

2) Do I feel hot/cute/professional in this item? (not necessarily all three at once, but if so, bonus!)

3) Am I just keeping this because someone bought it for me and if so, refer to question #1.

Then, I pushed all my clothes to one side of my drawer or I put the hangers on the rack in reverse. If I wore the item, I then put it back on the hanger the correct way. After six months, I looked to see how many hangers were still facing the wrong way or how many clothes were still on that side of the drawer. Those items were GONE unless it was something special like a cocktail dress or a costume piece that I wouldn't necessarily wear every six months. I inspired my husband to do the same and we go through our closets at least quarterly. I still use the reverse hanger technique every season.

Magazines/Books/CDs. I used to love to look at magazines and made the mistake of cashing in Delta points that were going to expire, but were not enough to use for a flight, for magazines. I think at one point I was getting about 10. The ones that arrived weekly, like TIME or Newsweek, did nothing but cause me anxiety. If they started stacking up I felt behind because 'Yikes! They are current events! I have to read them now!". I also subscribed to fashion, fitness magazines, home, and cooking magazines. When I made the decision to get rid of all of them, it was partially because I couldn't keep up and partially because I wanted to stop being subjected to advertisements. We had gotten rid of our cable and have only had Netflix (not even rabbit ears) for over five years now. I haven't missed the advertisements at all. I had read a book about the psychology of advertising and decided I no longer wanted to be infected more than I would be just living my life. I have to say that my quest for new things really has decreased tremendously since I no longer have TV or get magazines.

I donated or sold all of the books I had already read and wouldn't read again and now I probably have fewer than ten books in my house total because I have a Kindle. I would ask myself if I was keeping the book to 'look smarter', 'more well-read', etc. I wanted to only have things that were 1) beautiful or interesting, 2) functional 3) sentimental (but only to me and that were *truly* sentimental).

Compact discs were easy. We rip everything to our computers so we can listen on our phones or iPods so all but signed copies were donated. Eventually, I even donated my signed copies because I'm not someone who sees the value in a name written on an item. It might mean much more to someone else.

Toiletries. Being a business traveler, I accumulated a LOT of toiletries. If I used the shampoo one time at a hotel, I would bring it home with me so I had bags of toiletries. It is such a wasteful part of hotels because they throw all of those little bottles away daily. Millions of them. I felt like I was at least doing my part and would either use them myself or put them aside to donate to our annual Holidays and Hygiene party where admission price is a bag of hygiene products for Haven House. One thing I started doing was asking the hotel not to replenish the toiletries so if they cleaned my room, they didn't put another set out even though I had only used the first one once. Then, I sucked it up and only took the products home that I would actually buy.

More Habit Changes. Put all my kitchen gear in a box and if I hadn't used it within six months –bye-bye! Decluttered my sports gear, downsized my home and moved into a smaller townhome with yard work covered by the HOA.

Steps for Behaviour Change

What does this have to do with business travel? For the most part, being productive and healthy at home is much easier so it may have to start there. Then it can move to when you travel. Behavior change starts with a plan and we will discuss the specific steps later in the book. Consider the following when you determine what it is you want to plan and what kind of behavior or habit you want to incorporate into your life.

1. What are your goals?

    a. Who do you want to be?

    b. How do you want to look?

    c. What do you want to feel?

2. What's your whine?

    a. What is your excuse?

    b. Who or what is standing in your way (or who/what do you perceive is standing in your way?)

3. What's your win?

    a. What kind of resources do you have?

    b. Who can help you or hold you accountable?

4. What's your plan?

    a. Specific

    b. Measureable

    c. Attainable

    d. Realistic

    e. Timely

How to Use This Book

I don't want you to just 'survive' at travel. I want you to master it. At the very least, arrive home with enough energy and time left that you can spend time with the people you love and do the tasks at home that need taking care of. Basically, ignore what has become the conventional method to just give up and give in when traveling. Read through the book in its entirety or pick a section you want to learn about and improve on. Then, pick one and ONLY one habit to change in each area at a time. Adding a behavior is typically much easier than removing a behavior. By adding a behavior, you may end up removing another without much work. For example, by adding more vegetables, I automatically removed less healthy foods. Start with the simplest changes first, choosing only one at a time, and then after you have declared victory and it is a permanent behavior change, find another one to try out.

For ease of reading I'll refer to business travelers, road warriors and mobile professionals as mobile pros throughout the rest of the book. I've divided up the sections into the six key areas but keep in mind that some will overlap and others will apply to all sections.

Step 1 – Air Travel

Carlson Wagonlit Travel has done the most extensive research to date on approximately 6,000 travelers. Stressors were categorized and rated. One of the high stressors for females was 'routine breakers' and included not being able to eat healthy meals. Even for those times when our menu is chosen for us, we can still do some things to help us take control. Eating on the road can be tough, especially when your sphere of control is small, like in a business-meeting situation. You can be healthy but you do have to plan well and be flexible. I'll go over a few different scenarios and give you some tips to help you through them.

Airport Nutrition (is that an oxymoron?)

The dreaded airport. Land of fast food, processed food and little variety. Larger airports typically have enough options that almost everyone can find something. The hard ones are really small regional airports. I have walked miles up and down terminals trying to figure out what is the 'least bad' thing I can get. This is where a great app can be super helpful. One that I like is iFly. The app has a wealth of information but what I use most is the listing of restaurants and cafes that are in each terminal so I can plan appropriately. If you have this app you can check ahead of time and know if there is something for you to eat during your connection. If not, you may need to get something at your first airport or on your way to the airport or even take something with you from home if it is your first leg.

A few years ago the Physician's Committee for Responsible Medicine (PCRM) started rating major airports for healthy meal choices. Their criteria were that the airport had to offer *one* low-fat, high-fiber, cholesterol-free vegetarian entrée. This is not per terminal but per airport! This is really abysmal and offering only one should be given a big fat **F** in my book but at least they are starting somewhere. Given the minimal standards of one of these meals it is very disappointing to see that only 76% of 18 of the busiest airports even offered *one*!

The top five for healthy choices, according to PCRM are

1) Newark Liberty

2) Las Vegas McCarran

3) Detroit Metro Wayne County

4) Houston George Bush

5) A tie between Chicago O'Hare, Miami, Orlando, Washington-Dulles and Phoenix Sky Harbor.

The worst was Hartsfield-Jackson Atlanta airport. Having connected there many times, I am not surprised.

At the airport, look for foods that are the least processed. No matter what nutrition plan you are following; Paleo, vegetarian, low-sodium, low-fat, 40/30/30 - the one common denominator is the lack of processed foods. Show me a nutrition plan that tells you to eat more processed food and I will show you a unicorn crapping rainbows. If your food is minimally processed, more often than not it will be naturally low in sodium. The air pressure on the plane and the act of sitting for so long and moving very little causes you to retain fluids. Sodium exacerbates that. How many people have gotten a little constipated after flying? There lies the problem. It happens to the best of us.

Most flights do not offer meals anymore so this would mostly apply to international flights but it is important to know that you can choose low-sodium, vegetarian, low-fat and low-calorie meals as long as you choose at least 24 hours in advance via the airline's website.

Did you know that altitude affects our taste buds? Airlines have to add more salt to the food in order for it to taste good. This means you are taking in an excessive amount of sodium, which when combined with the lack of movement, will make your body retain water in your blood vessels. This is why your ankles swell and your pants may feel too tight. Altitude also affects your digestive system causing gases to expand by as much as 30 percent. Another reason not to have carbonated beverages on board.

The typical airline meal has 950 calories, which is half an average woman's daily caloric intake. Think about it...if you are eating a meal served on an airplane, then you are probably on a very long flight and not expending many calories that day. You just ate half of them in one not-so-tasty meal!

The humidity falls to about 20% in a cabin (as opposed to 40-70 percent or if you live in the South East in the summer, 90%!). You may not get dehydrated much on a short flight but if you have ever experienced dry eyes, nose or throat, or saw blood in your tissue when you blew your noggin, this is due to the dry air in the cabin. The last thing you want is a high-sodium meal making you retain fluids and worsening the problem.

Buy plain water or decaf coffee or tea. Try to avoid having caffeine on the plane or make sure you drink a lot of water as well. The carbonated, sugary or artificially sweetened sodas they serve on the plane won't do anything to help you get through your trip. I love to have a latte or tea in flight out of habit, so I have switched to decaf.

It's also much safer to purchase your water, coffee or tea before you board as aircraft have been under scrutiny for testing positive for e-coli in the coffee, water and ice! A little poo with your beverage?

Grab and Go Coolers

Be careful when purchasing food from the grab and go coolers, especially if you are buying a meat product. Inspections records for almost 800 restaurants at 10 airports found violations. A review of 35 restaurants at Reagan National Airport revealed that 77% of the restaurants had at least one CRITICAL violation. Critical violations included: Meat stored too warm; raw meat contaminating ready-to-eat food; rodent droppings (there's that poo again), kitchen's lacking soap (poo on hands?). Yuck.

If you are purchasing from a grab and go cooler, be sure to eat the food right away and not let it sit in your bag for an hour to eat on the plane. Also consider that your items with ingredients such as mayonnaise, eggs or meat may have already been at a low temperature. I've heard people complain that they ate something bad from the airport. In reality, it may have been okay but they bought it 20 minutes before boarding and then didn't start eating it until after they had taken off and the beverage cart had passed by. Their tuna salad sandwich that was 'bad' was sitting in room temperature conditions for over an hour before they ate it!

Foods to Avoid

Besides the Grab and Go Coolers, there are a few things you should avoid or consider as treats only. First are soft pretzels. When I first started traveling a decade ago and was a bad vegetarian, I lived on soft pretzels, protein bars, frozen yogurt and Frappucinos when I had to eat in airports.

Soft pretzels are 400-500 calories of bread with very little fiber. Since it is a simple carbohydrate you may as well treat it like a muffin. It will digest quickly and not do anything to make you feel full. Plus, you are usually getting it coated in butter or dipping it into some kind of sugary sauce. Ask for it with no salt to combat the dreaded plane bloat.

For Vegans who wish to treat themselves, Auntie Anne's pretzel mix for Original, Sweet Almond, Garlic, Jalapeno and Raisin pretzels do not contain animal, dairy or egg as long as you ask for it with no butter.

Frozen Yogurt is one of the most processed foods you can eat. It comes in a bag in liquid form. Don't let the brands that masquerade as 'healthy' fool you either. They either have a ton of sugar or are artificially sweetened. Let's take Pinkberry frozen yogurt as an example. The second ingredient is sugar and it has around 23 ingredients, one of which is artificial flavor. How can something that is marketed as healthy have so many ingredients? If you need a real treat, just get a single scoop of real ice cream.

Sugary coffee drinks have the quadruple whammy of sugar, caffeine, calories and sodium. A Grande Mocha Cookie Crumble Frappuccino with whip is 470 calories. A Berry Mocha Frappuccino has 570! These are dessert and should be treated like a milkshake. A treat to have on occasion, if at all.

Sauce-laden foods, like the kind you would get at one of the fast food 'Chinese' restaurants will be high in sodium and probably sugar, adding on a lot of calories as well. I've traveled to China and I can promise you that what we get here is completely bastardized and not Chinese at all. You can usually get steamed mixed vegetables so I would go for those and whatever has the least amount of sauce on it.

Raw fish sushi may not be stored properly so be careful if it is in a grab and go cooler. Otherwise, sushi can be healthy, just make sure it is prepared fresh or buy a vegetarian roll.

Processed meats like deli meats and hot dogs will be very high in sodium. It is common for a typical airport sandwich to have an ENTIRE day's amount of sodium in it. Remember how sodium+dehydration+lack of movement = an entire section of The USA Today on the toilet?

Lastly, the giant muffins, scones and cookies. These are usually 3-4 servings a piece! I used to get a giant cookie (about 370 calories) when I traveled and the way I weaned myself through behavior change is I would tear off some of it and immediately throw the rest away. I didn't care about the money waste because it wasn't my money since I was on a per diem and I was still able to get my fix.

What to Choose

If you are vegetarian, you may get lucky and be in an airport with great salads that you can add beans, hummus, fruit and nuts to. If I am leaving from home, I'll put some frozen edamame in a bag or container and let it thaw naturally to snack on. Good luck finding organic, non-GMO tofu, even at the 'Asian' restaurants but at least you can get some steamed mixed vegetables. *Why do I put Asian in quotes? Because we tend to ruin everything here and the food is not even remotely close to what it would really be like.* If I know I am going to be eating in an airport I try to make sure I get good protein sources at my meals before I go to the airport or when I get to my destination. If you eat fish and there are real sit-down restaurants you can usually find salmon. I would stay away from the mayo-laden tuna salad sandwiches, especially if they are in a grab and go cooler.

Meat eaters who aren't picky have it the easiest at airports because you can always find a grilled chicken breast. However, I have never seen antibiotic or hormone-free meats at an airport so depending on your food rules, you may have to opt for plant-based meals.

- Hummus

- Edamame

- Salads (careful with dressings, meats and eggs unless fresh)

- Steamed mixed vegetables

- Non-meat sushi

- Salmon – wild is preferred over farmed

- Grilled chicken – ideally this is organic, hormone and antibiotic free

Gluten-Free

Because I have Hashimoto's Disease I have a very strict gluten-free diet. I cannot have it, ever. Not even a molecule of it. Airport chains that have gluten-free options include California Pizza Kitchen, Chili's, and Wolfgang Puck Express. Always double check with the staff even if you are ordering a salad or vegetables because they may have been cooked in a sauce with gluten or be contaminated in some other way.

> *No matter what the news and your favorite magazines say, gluten affects more autoimmune diseases than just Celiac and the research has been out there for at least a decade. Stay tuned for my next book on Hack the Hashimoto's Lifestyle!*

Cheap airport packing

I am actually really cheap at the airport if I am going on a personal trip and a business isn't paying for it. I refuse to pay $9.00 for a crudité cup or $6.00 for a small fruit cup. When I am traveling for personal reasons I plan ahead and make sure I pack a sandwich, fruit and vegetables. One thing I have recently discovered is that I can take single serving packs of hummus and Wholly Guacamole in my liquids bag. I freeze them overnight and just let them thaw in the bag. Perfect to snack on and just the right size! I also take my own reusable coffee mug so that my drink stays hot and I am less likely to spill it. Then I just ask for hot water and I have my own tea.

Airplane Hygiene

Airplanes are a breeding ground for what ails you because they are hardly ever disinfected. I have no shame in my game and am not embarrassed to pull out a disinfectant wipe on the plane to wipe down the seatbelt, headrest, armrests and lap tray. Bacteria that have been found on tray tables include e-coli, streptococcus and staphylococcus. Once I saw a woman put her shoes on the tray table. Gross. I also don't put any food in the magazine pouch. I have seen poopy diapers and leftover food from previous travelers. Think about how quickly planes are boarded after the previous flight. They are just picking up visible trash, that's all. If you are sitting near a window, wipe down the window with your wipe. Who knows how many heads have been leaning against that window? If you go to the bathroom, don't touch anything with your bare hands. Pick up a tissue and use it to touch everything. When you get back to your seat, use alcohol sanitizer. You don't need antibacterial sanitizer. Plain alcohol sanitizer is much better and is enough to kill most germs and viruses. Bring your own magazines, especially if it is at the end of the month and hundreds of hands have touched that magazine. Seriously, do you really need to buy a $300 watering bowl with a fountain for your pooch?

Jet Lag

Jet lag is not in your head. It is a real physiological phenomenon and is even worse when traveling on international or long haul flights. According to CWT, lost time and productivity for international flights is approximately 15.6 hours. Unfortunately, most companies don't consider cost-benefit when choosing to fly economy, business or first-class. If the traveler is stressed, tired, non-productive or exhausted how well will they perform? If they haven't been able to work any during their flight, now they also are behind in their work and have to make up for it when they get to their destination.

Symptoms of jet lag include:

- Fatigue

- Insomnia

- Loss of appetite

- Reduced concentration

- Reduced fitness capacity

- Nausea

- GI distress (also caused by altitude)

- Joint swelling and stiffness (also caused by altitude)

- Muscle pain and stiffness

The hypothalamus regulates our sleep cycles, temperature and appetite. It responds slowly to changes in external time and light levels. It is estimated that it takes one full day of recovery for every one hour of time difference. Traveling east is harder than traveling west. Think about it…it is much easier to stay awake in the evening then wake up three or five hours earlier. If you live in San Diego and you are doing business in Raleigh-Durham and you normally get up at 6am, you are now getting up at 3am and are expected to perform your best.

No matter how experienced you are as a road warrior, jet lag affects you. It still affects pilots and flight attendants even after years of travel, they just get more used to the feelings. If you are traveling across several time zones you may need to give yourself an extra day or two to mentally and physically prepare for your meeting or event. You could still work but maybe not meet with a client. Better yet, take a day or two as vacation and see some sights and then start your meeting.

The Argonne Diet Protocol was developed by Charles Ehret of the US Department of Energy Argonne National Laboratory and has been shown to help reduce the effects of jet lag. It was designed to help travelers and shift workers who have to rotate work hours. It was tested and found that those who managed to complete it were 7 - 16 times less likely to experience jet lag! Unfortunately, it is hard to follow and isn't much fun because it involves alternate feasting and fasting for up to four days before travel. It also involves no eating on the plane and if I am on a super long flight, eating on the plane helps to break up the monotony and I look forward to it. If you want the full diet, go to http://www.netlib.org/misc/jet-lag-diet

The modified Argonne Anti-Jet-Lag Diet Protocol would be to eat a normal breakfast and lunch the day you travel then fast right before and during your flight, only drinking water. As soon as you land you have a meal at the normal time for that time zone then continue to eat at local times. The fasting should occur for 14-24 hours. Breakfast should be high protein and dinners should be high carbohydrate and very low protein. Caffeinated beverages should only be consumed between 3-5pm local time. Personally, I have not tried this because again, I like to eat, but for those of you that wish to try it, let me know how it goes!

Exercise

This is VERY important to help with jet lag. Exercise can affect our circadian rhythms as well and if exercise can be done outdoors during daylight that is even better. Light + movement tells the body 'Wake up!' If you exercise at 6:30am at home, try to exercise at 6:30am in whatever time zone you are in. Keep in mind that your body has gone through a lot and it is a biological process so you may not be running that eight-minute mile with the same ease or performing your bench press with the same amount of weight. This is especially true if you go from low altitude to high altitude. The first time I ran on a treadmill in Mexico City I thought I was ill because I was running so slow. I didn't realize I was at 8000 feet! If I am on a short domestic trip with a time difference of only 1-2 hours, I try to maintain my home schedule and get up and go to bed at the same time.

Supplementation

Melatonin is synthesized from the amino acid tryptophan. It is a hormone that controls circadian rhythm and is secreted by the pineal gland in the brain. It is released at night in the dark. This is one reason why watching screens like laptops can affect your sleep. It is preventing melatonin from being released. Studies are inconsistent on whether it helps with jet lag but if you do choose to try it, dose timing is important. You should wait until you land in your new time zone to supplement. Studies suggest taking .5mg to 5mg of melatonin for three nights, one hour before normal bedtime, after you have reached your destination. If the trip is short, just a couple of days, melatonin won't really do much for you. Placebo effect? Never hurts!

Airport Meetings

Taking meetings in airports is discouraged if you can help it, unless you can find somewhere quiet to talk. It can be distracting to the person on the receiving end because of the announcements being made. You could be speaking about something that is confidential and not realize who is listening. In addition, most people talk too loud on their cell phones and it is *annoying*. Cell phones are very good devices now and I don't know why people continue to shout or talk loudly into them. On planes, if you are sitting on the tarmac waiting to take off, you can actually whisper into your phone and I can almost promise the person you are speaking to on the other end will hear you. Please be considerate of others and talk softly. **No one** thinks your conversation is as important as you do, even if you are a CEO, a celebrity or a Chicago Bull.

Luggage Types

There are so many different luggage types, and pros and cons to each kind that it often comes down to personal choice. However, I'll provide some info you may not think of before purchasing. High-quality luggage is a necessity if you are a business traveler. This isn't the time to go to Wal-Mart and get the $25.00 bag. This is not where 'good enough' comes into play. You'll regret it when you are running down the terminal with your luggage case flopping along and your handle breaks.

Tumi is my carry-on of choice for the last seven years. The company is very high quality and has a stellar reputation. My mistake? I bought a case that is a peachy coral color thinking that it would be easy to spot and wouldn't be accidentally picked up by one of the other 5,000 black bag carrying people in the airport. The first time I checked that beautiful piece of luggage it came back streaked with black and incredibly dirty. I have never been able to get the stains out so for years I have strolled around with my dirty looking Tumi bag. It is almost unfortunate they are made so well because I am too frugal to switch it out when the only thing wrong with it is cosmetic. Lesson learned – consider the color and if it is easy to clean.

Even though I wish I hadn't bought that particular color, I do not regret purchasing something other than black. It is just too easy to accidentally pick up someone else's bag. I recommend using a colorful luggage tag. I have seen people tie ribbons or string onto their bag but I have also seen these ribbons torn to shreds in the conveyor belt. Once I had to wait 30 extra minutes for my baggage because someone's ribbon clogged up the machine.

Consider the wheels. If you were of the inline skating generation, you probably know the difference between a cheap set of wheels and a quality set. Same thing here. You want your wheels to roll smoothly and evenly. Try to get a bag with four 360-degree wheels instead of a two-wheeled case. They are much easier to get down the aisle and you can pull it beside instead of behind you. With four wheels it is less likely to fall over due to the weight. My husband's bag does that and it drives us crazy. He rarely travels so we haven't replaced it but it is usually the sign of a cheap bag.

Look for an add-a-bag system if you frequently use a laptop or smaller carry-on. This typically consists of a hook or sleeve so you can attach the smaller piece to the larger piece and pull with one hand. Some luggage even has a strap to attach your coat.

Hard case vs. Soft case. Hard cases used to be super heavy but they helped protect your belongings and got less beat up in checked baggage. Now they are made of much lighter material so I would consider it, however check the material to make sure it isn't easy to scratch, like some polycarbonate. Hard cases are also less attractive to bed bugs. My preference is softer, expandable cases with a few pockets but not too many. If I have too many pockets, I forget where I put things. I would also try to find a fabric that is washable yet water-repellant.

The largest suitcase I have fits in an overhead bin on most jets. Be very careful you don't buy one too big if that is what you plan on doing with it. Whatever size bag you buy, you will fill it. On one trip that lasted a month, I used my Tumi carry-on and a backpack. I can't imagine a time when I would need a full-size suitcase. Your case of choice should also be light enough that you can lift it. Do some shoulder presses with it in the store for a quickie workout (☺) and to see if it is so big that it is awkward to lift over your head. Bags from Eagle Creek have interior compression wings to help you get more of your stuff inside and some of their cases integrate with their Pack-It system. If I were looking at luggage to replace my Tumi, I would seriously consider some of their bags.

A quality telescoping extended handle is a sign of a good bag. If you have ever struggled with your luggage handle you know what it is like to have one that doesn't push down or pull up easily. This should be effortless. Make sure you walk around the store with it to ensure that the handle is long enough you don't hit your heel. If you are short, like me, you want to make sure that the handle isn't so long you are dragging it four feet behind you and annoying your fellow travelers. If the handle is built inside the bag, it will take up more space and make it more likely to fall over.

Packing

I feel I am a pretty efficient packer. For the three weeks I spent training clients in California with only a carry-on and a backpack, I had exercise and dress clothes, casual clothes, a pair of boots, dress shoes, sneakers, a SMRT-Core and a collapsible hoop! I still could have probably packed less and have found in the last couple of years that I almost always can get away with deleting 1-2 things in my suitcase. When my husband and I went to NYC for three days we each took a small backpack and that was it. It was so nice not to have to lug roller bags through the subway or along the sidewalks.

One thing I believe helps a lot as far as packing is using an Eagle Creek Pack-It folder. I have bought these as gifts for family members and recommend them to anyone that travels. They help keep your clothes from wrinkling but also provide compression so you can fit more into your suitcase. They come in different sizes so make sure you buy one that will fit your particular suitcase. Use any available space or holes. I stuff socks inside sneakers, exercise clothes inside my SMRT-Core, belts inside shoes, etc.

I have duplicate toiletries so I rarely forget to pack my toothbrush, face wash, etc. I just leave all of my toiletries in my bag. When I traveled weekly, I even bought two containers of makeup so I didn't even have to repack that. Some people also just have one makeup bag or toiletry kit so they just swap it out each time. The main thing to discourage is doing a hybrid approach where you keep some things in your luggage and other things in your bathroom at home. It's too easy to forget an item. However, if you do forget, most hotels will give you razors, toothbrushes and toothpaste for free at the desk.

I have sneakers that I consider my travel sneakers so I'm never without and there is no excuse to dismiss my exercise routine when I am on the road. If you don't want to pack sneakers, you can still get a good workout in your room barefoot. Not all routines require footwear.

Since shoes take up a lot of real estate, I try to have my clothes one-color theme per trip so I either need brown or black shoes. I try to get shoes that can work dressed up or business casual. Regardless, if you are a woman and you wear high heels, you should always have some kind of slip-on shoe or low-heeled shoe in the airport. I'm not talking about the 1980s white Reeboks with business suit look, but running through an airport in heels can be dangerous! I actually saw someone break an ankle doing this. It was awful for her and I am sure very painful physically and emotionally. Plus, not everyone can run like Carrie Bradshaw and any chiropractor or podiatrist would tell you that you are seriously messing with your biomechanics doing that.

I try to buy wrinkle-free clothes along with the similar color schemes. If you are male, you could wear the same suit two days in a row and most people wouldn't notice as long as you changed your tie, however a suit definitely takes up more space in your luggage. Female clothing tends to be a little more distinctive so we might have to mix it up, but can definitely still wear the same color scheme and bring along a scarf or some other accessory. If I am visiting more than one client in a week, I re-wear my clothes all the time. Unless I sweat in them, which is doubtful if it is a business meeting, I take one pair of black pants and wear those twice and take two tops and one jacket. So much easier. I call clothes that are a little dirty (one wearing sweat and stain-free) but clean enough to wear again, my clerty clothes (clean/dirty). My best friend, who is also a business traveler, used to pack a new pair of black pants for every day of the week she traveled. She now has downsized her packing *and* her dry cleaning bill.

There have been some great experiments on clothing and what other people notice. Basically, most people notice little if you re-wear items that are neutrals or classics. This especially works with pants and skirts. Again, for guys, the tie is the thing people will notice, but only if it is a bright color or print. Unless your job is in fashion, you don't have to stand out. I have always been complimented on my clothes so I feel like the neutral, wrinkle-free wardrobe with some fun or colorful accessory or shirt works great!

Suits - I'm so sorry gentleman. I do not envy having to pack a suit. One way to keep a suit jacket from getting wrinkled is to wear it on the plane but not all men want to travel with their suit jacket on. Some flight attendants will allow you to hang them in the closet. There are many great videos on how to pack a suit online. www.businessinsider.com has a great one that I recommend.

Packing Lists

Any list making app will work to make a packing list. Whatever list making app you use, it needs to be something you can check off and then remove the checks *each* time you pack for a trip. It is so easy to forget one little item and even after all this time, I still use a checklist. I have a packing list for vacation, camping, racing, and business. I consider everything I will be doing: Traveling, Business Dinner, Business Meeting, afternoon of sight-seeing (sometimes it really does happen!), Exercise, Travel Home. I also think about the activities I will be doing while on that particular trip – standing a lot? Walking around a hospital for an hour? The client is a 10-block walk from my hotel? All of these things come into play so every trip will be a little bit different. This is what my latest checklist had, but it certainly varies depending on the trip and the climate. An * denotes having a spare packed at all times.

Business Trip Sample List

CLOTHES

☐ *Casual or travel outfit* - Needs to be comfortable but *cannot* be pajamas. Seriously, if you are over the age of six, you should never ever, *ever* be wearing your pajamas in the airport. My heart rate is going up right now thinking of you in your big flannel pants. You can be comfy without wearing PJs. **Don't do it.** During travel I usually wear jeans, cargos (convenient at the airport) or very stylish yoga-style pants. If I have a bulky jacket or sweater, I'll wear it so that it saves room in my suitcase.

☐ *Business clothes for each day* - Streamline by wearing the same color scheme and not packing bulky items. I stopped buying shirts that require ironing because I like ironing about as much as I like picking lint out of someone else's toenails. I also liken the sound of an ironing board unfolding to a woman screaming in terror so I try not to use them.

☐ *Sweater or jacket* – Versatile and wrinkle-free for cold planes and meeting rooms.

☐ *Underwear**

☐ *Bra* (if applicable) – Consider the cuts of your tops to determine what type you need.

☐ *Dress Socks, hose or tights**

☐ *Tie (if applicable)**

☐ *Dress shoes*

☐ *Belt* - Reversible belts are great to save space

☐ *Coat*

☐ *Hat/gloves/scarf* – If you live somewhere warm and travel frequently to colder climates, keep a spare pair of cheap gloves in your bag. A big scarf or hat is great to have in your carry-on because you can use it as a pillow or to wrap around your head on the plane.

□ *Pajamas* - I sometimes sleep in my exercise clothes to save space. In the winter I make sure I at least have pajama pants because I never know about the temperature control in the room.

EXERCISE

□ *Sports Bra* (if applicable)*

□ *Workout Clothes* - Wicking clothes are important so they dry a little before you repack them. If you are working out in your room just wear your underclothes and a sports bra (if applicable) and save the luggage space! Use the hotel dry cleaning bag for your used workout clothes to separate them from any other clothes.

□ *Athletic socks**

□ *Sneakers** – lower profile saves room in your bag.

□ **Sprigs Wrist Banjee** – This holds my iPhone and hotel key while I'm working out and my ID and credit card when I am traveling.

□ *Exercise equipment* – Depends on where I am staying and for how long: Travel Yoga Mat, SMRT-Core, **Jetsetter Rubberbanditz**™ or collapsible hoop.

□ *Road ID*

TOILETRIES

All of these should be a second set that never leaves your suitcase. Check Environmental Working Group ewg.org to find products rated 0-2. These products have less toxic substances you are putting on your body, your hair or in your mouth.

☐ *Comb/brush**

☐ *shampoo, conditioner, soap** - I almost always just use whatever is at the hotel to save space. This is only packed if I don't know the hotel or don't like what they offer.

☐ *hair product**

☐ *Face Wash** - Yes To Cucumbers Soothing Hypoallergenic Facial Towelettes (facial cleanser) is rated a 1 by ewg.org and it isn't a liquid!

☐ *Face lotion** – Badger Damascus Rose SPF 15 is rated 0 and smells delicious. Jason Fragrance Free Facial Cream is also rated 0.

☐ *Sunblock** – if applicable

☐ *Deodorant**

☐ *Hand sanitizer** - Don't get the antibacterial kind! Check ewg.org to find one rated 0-2.

☐ *Toothpaste, toothbrush and floss** - I love Tom's of Maine fennel and cinnamon clove - both rated 1.

☐ *Makeup** - Either buy duplicates or have one bag with all your makeup. I advise against having a hybrid system where you have some things duplicates and others not.

☐ *Hand lotion or balm** - I love Aquaphor. It's cheap, rated 1-2 by EWG and can be used as lip balm as well.

☐ *Feminine essentials* (if applicable)* – Some things you never want to be without ☺

☐ *Razor**

MEDICATION/FOOD

☐ *Vitamins/prescriptions**

☐ *Snacks**

☐ *Protein Powder** – I love <u>Vega</u> or Raw products.

☐ *Sports Nutrition** - gels (must pack in carry-on liquids bag), powdered sports drink, blocks/chomps or pitted dates. Hotels always carry Gatorade or PowerAde but both of these have artificial flavors, colors and sweeteners. Stay away!

☐ *Travel Mug and/or Water Bottle** – Besides the environmental impact, they keep hot drinks hot, cold drinks cold and you are less likely to spill your coffee on the plane.

LOGISTICS

☐ *Purse, wallet or utility belt, Sprigs Wrist Banjee*

☐ *Credit Cards/Cash* – Always have at least ten dollars in cash so you don't panic at unexpected tolls or get to the hotel and realize your only choice is to valet park and you haven't any money to tip. A dollar in quarters is also handy for parking meters.

☐ *Passport/ID*

☐ *Tickets* – downloaded onto phone or printed

☐ *GPS* – directions loaded

ELECTRONICS

☐ *Phone*

☐ *Laptop*

☐ *Phone charger** - I keep a spare cord in my laptop bag. If you do forget your charger, always ask at the hotel desk. They are the #1 most forgotten item so you may be able to snag one since most people don't have it shipped from the hotel.

☐ *Laptop charger/spare cord** – it is worth buying a spare cord when you buy your laptop so you don't have to crawl under your desk every time you leave to travel.

☐ *eReader (Kindle, Nook)*

☐ *Headphones** – keep a spare pair of cheap ones in your luggage or laptop bag in case you forget your good ones.

MISCELLANEOUS

☐ *Umbrella*

☐ *Mini First Aid Kit**

☐ *Sunglasses*

☐ *Hand Warmers/Toe Warmers** – I have Raynaud's Disease so I always keep packets in my suitcase.

☐ *Sleep Sack/Liner**

☐ *Sandwich Bags** – a few for extra food or in case something leaks.

I try not to check luggage unless I have a long layover. If I do have a substantial layover, I want to be able to walk around the airport. Lugging a roller bag and a laptop bag will prevent me from doing that as easily. Whether I check luggage or not, I always have a second bag on the plane with my laptop. Inside *that* bag I have a sealable bag with all of my liquids and my **Grid-It** with all of my peripherals attached to it. I love the Grid-It because I can pull everything out at once. I don't carry a big purse so everything goes in this bag. I use a wristlet or a **Sprigs Banjee** for my money, credit cards and phone.

Having a suitcase half-packed all the time is such a timesaver. I'm good at packing and always have everything ready in advance. What I am *not* good at is unpacking. I make myself unpack 25 things before I sit down to do anything. The number is arbitrary but it means that it is most of my bag so I end up finishing anyway. Otherwise, it can sit there for a week, half unpacked. We live in a three story house and the first room is my office so I put all my office stuff away, carry my suitcase to the middle floor and unpack travel mugs or water bottles and any food I have with me, then up to the top floor where I throw my clothes in the laundry. No matter what time I get home, I have to do 25 things because I am the world's laziest unpacker.

Security

I try to be fast through security by preparing before I leave home or when I turn in my rental car. If I'm leaving from home, I'll just pack my belt and jacket until I get through security and then I'll put it on. I try to wear shoes that are easy to get on and off (but still comfy). Since I usually wear a Sprigs Banjee when I travel, my phone, ID and credit card are on my wrist and I can pull it off easily. My liquids and laptop are removed from the bag. I put my items in the bin in reverse order of what I will be retrieving them in and I always put my shoes last. Why? Because I will not leave security without my shoes and this ensures nothing gets left behind. A great tip from smartwomantravelers.com is to remember PLLS Purse Laptop Liquids Shoes.

If I'm wearing sandals or heels without socks I'll try to remember to have some socks handy in my carry-on so I don't have to step barefoot through security. It's so gross. When I forget socks, I try to think happy, fungus-free thoughts.

Always watch the bins go through the scanner prior to going through security. If you send it through too early, someone could accidentally (or intentionally) take your things. In the rush of getting everything together, it is easy to forget something. If you do, you have to contact Transportation Security Administration Lost and Found. If you leave something in the airport at the gate, terminal or parking garage, contact the airport Lost and Found. If you leave an item on the plane, contact the airlines directly. I keep a business card in all my coat pockets and bags to make it easier for people to contact me if I have left something.

Having a photo of your luggage is a great idea in case it gets lost. You can send it to the airlines and it may help them to locate it. If I were packing something valuable I would take a photo of the inside as well. I make a habit of taking photo or video of everything in my home once per year and store it in the cloud. If there were ever a fire or theft, I would have proof of what I had for my insurance company.

Safety

Most business travel is done alone and often to unfamiliar areas. It's very important that someone know where you are when you are traveling. You can use an app like 'Find My Friend' or with TripIt, you can have someone you trust automagically copied on all your travel itineraries.

Your cell phone should have an ICE number – In Case of Emergency. I have ICE in the name of my husband and two girlfriends so that if something were to happen, the police or fire department could just search ICE instead of guessing whom I belonged to. If you are traveling outside of the country, always have your passport with you so they are able to call an embassy if necessary.

Be careful wearing flashy watches, jewelry or clothes, especially in a high crime area. Turn your expensive rings around to the palm of your hand in common areas. I remember when I was working in Buenos Aires and mentioned running along the river and a woman asked me if I ran with my ring on. Since I rarely take it off and would never consider leaving it in a hotel room, I stated I had. The class was horrified and said I should at least turn it to the inside. What I would have thought of as offensive was actually naive!

Step 2 – Hotels

Suitcase Essentials for Nutrition

In my suitcase I always keep protein powder. This is partly because I'm not always sure I'll get a good protein source in an airport or work meal, but it can also be mixed into so many things it just makes it simple as a back-up. I use single serving packets or put three servings into an infant formula container. I use Vega or Raw brands but there are several good ones on the market. I would check consumerlab.com or consumer reports to make sure your brand is high quality. It should be free of refined sugars, artificial sweeteners and isolates. When people get concerned about soy or whey, it is in the isolate form because it has basically been stripped away of all that is good and left with all that is bad! Protein powders can be mixed with cereal, yogurt, fruit, water or milk. I also keep the single serving bags of nuts, dried oats and some tea and instant coffee packets available. These things will keep for a long time so I don't have to worry and I always make sure I restock. Hotel pantries tend to be filled with junk food so I need to have something in my arsenal when I get there at 11:00pm and my only choices are a Luna bar, Dinty Moore Beef Stew and Lance crackers.

Exercise on the Road

Exercising on the road takes planning, discipline, flexibility and creativity. You may not be able to do your favorite activities but you can find a few things that you can travel with and are willing to do to maintain your health, weight, stress level and sanity! You are not always going to have the ideal gym or city to work out in. Get over it and stop with the excuses already!

Choosing a Hotel

When I am searching for places to stay, I always filter out the hotels without a fitness center if it is going to be cold, dark or in an area that isn't safe to walk or run outside. Then I check out the photos. Hotels are great at making fitness centers look 3x the size they really are, so unless it is obvious it is a really nice center, I call the site to ensure that the equipment actually *works*. The photo could be ten years old. If a hotel doesn't have a fitness center or it is really bad, you can ask if they provide passes to nearby gyms. Sometimes this is an even better deal.

*I used to stay at a Homewood Suites in Plano, Texas because they **didn't** have a fitness center. Instead, they gave passes to 24-Hour Fitness two blocks away. That, coupled with its location next to Whole Foods, made it my favorite place to travel for business!*

Hotels always seem to have their fitness centers right next to their pools, which means the rooms are very hot and humid. Even when they aren't next to pools I find that they keep them too warm. Make sure you bring wicking clothes and buy a bottle of water since you will definitely sweat more. It helps to go at 'off times' which means super early in the morning, late in the evening or during the day, which usually isn't likely when you are traveling for business. Always check the times the fitness center is open. Some hotels have them closed until 6 or 7am, which is a big fat **F** in my book. This basically says 'We don't care or know anything about business travelers!'

One morning I was in the hotel fitness center and started running on the treadmill. I started smelling this awful odor and could not figure out what it was. A man walked into the center and took one sniff and walked out. Then a second one came in and kept looking around trying to determine what the horrid smell was. The smell kept getting worse but I wasn't going to stop running. I knew it smelled familiar but I couldn't figure it out. The guy was so disgusted he finally gave me a nasty look and left. I didn't realize until I got back to the hotel room that the smell was ME! Why did I smell so bad? I flew home later that night and was putting laundry into the washer when I realized what had happened. My cat Pele (pre happy-medication) was not fond of me traveling at the time and we were having issues with him peeing on clothes if we left them on the floor. The little bastard had peed on my workout clothes and I was wearing them! As I was running and heating up, the smell got worse. If you are 'that guy' that had to deal with the smell of cat urine, because there is no smell like it, I apologize profusely, especially since I still got a good workout in! I joke that nothing, not even being covered in cat pee, can stop me from getting a run in. However, I do NOT recommend it for motivation!

Explore

If you feel you are in an area that is safe, run or walk outside. Hotels will often have routes at their desk you can pick up, or look up routes using different apps or websites. WalkJogRunning is 2.99 and has over 600,000 running routes that other users have submitted. Runkeeper enables you to track your run or walk via GPS and you can share your information if you want to via Twitter or Facebook. For safety reasons, I would be careful doing this if you don't want others to know that you aren't home and if you have a lot of friends or Twitter followers and your information is public.

Even if I work out in the morning, I will typically go for a walk outside to explore or even on the treadmill in the evening just to get some movement after a long day sitting on a plane or in meetings. You don't always have to sweat. Just put your sneakers on and walk leisurely. If there is a free treadmill, I will walk while reading the paper or a book. It's not fast enough to get sweaty but I still get some movement in. However, if the fitness center is busy, I don't do this. It wouldn't be fair to the people *really* trying to exercise.

The first time I went to Sao Paulo, Brazil for business I stayed near Ibirapuera Park, the Central Park of Sao Paulo. I didn't know how big the park was or if I would get lost in it (not that big and I never got lost) so when I saw a running group in matching shirts I ran up to them and asked if I could join them. I don't speak Portuguese and they didn't speak great English but we understood each other enough that I figured out they were going about 10k, which was perfect.

We took off and the men's group ran ahead of the women's group. My nose runs like a faucet sometimes and it was one of those days. I discreetly blew a snot rocket, aka Farmer's Blow, aka Marcey Blow (my husband's name for it because I taught him how to do it!). Well, the women immediately stopped and looked at me and started talking very fast in Portuguese. I thought 'Uh, oh. I have created a major cultural faux pas.' Much to my surprise, they wanted me to teach them how to do it! Turns out they had often tried but ended up snotting down their legs. I showed them how to do it properly, they practiced and were happy, and away we went!

Towards the end of the run we were back up with the guys and one of the women blew a perfect rocket to the side in the grass. Three of the men looked at her with horror on their faces. I couldn't tell what she was saying but it was something to the effect of 'This American woman taught us how to do it!' Thankfully, the lack of Portuguese was helpful at this point because whatever the men were saying to me, I don't think I want to know. I considered my work complete as I had now empowered a lovely group of Brazilian women to get rid of the sniffs and go on with the rockets!

In Room Exercise

I usually try to stay in a 'suites' type hotel like Embassy Suites, Springhill Suites, Homewood Suites, etc. This way I have extra space to exercise in my room to do Yoga, videos, resistance bands, and portable suspension systems like TRX. All of which are perfectly suitable for Underwear Workouts!

If you don't like to pack a lot or you have forgotten your exercise clothes, you can work out in your room in your underwear and no one will know the difference! Some great apps or YouTube channels are YJMag by Yoga Journal, Ekhartyoga.com or YogaAmazing. These are great for the end of the day when you feel like you need to stretch out or you just want to do something without getting too sweaty. Between meeting time and dinner I go to my room, strip down, do a 15-20 minute yoga series, put my clothes back on and go to dinner. I feel so much better, I am stretched out from sitting all day and I don't have to shower. There are definitely harder videos you can choose from and bodyweight workouts where you don't need any equipment. I offer several short workouts myself at www.marceyrader.com. If you sign up for a program with me I can tailor it to whatever equipment you travel with!

Portable equipment that I like to take includes:

- Resistance bands – lightweight and take up very little space. I prefer Rubberbanditz brand and designed my own kit for mobile professionals called the Jetsetter www.jetsettergymkit.com. You will not be disappointed.

- Tennis ball for self-myofascial release. SMR is a stretching technique using a foam roller, ball or other assistive device and helps improve flexibility, muscle recovery, and movement efficiency, inhibit overactive muscles and reduce pain.

- SMRT-Core that I can double up and use for SMR and core exercises.

- Collapsible hoop – yep, I'm a hoopdancer!

- Ultimate Sandbag if I am traveling by car.

- TRX suspension system.

Another time when I was in Sao Paulo, Brazil I took my collapsible hoop to Ibirapuera Park. I put on my headphones and iPod Shuffle and started practicing and dancing. Quite a few people would stop to watch me, smile and clap. I consider myself an advanced beginner so I'm not great by any means but I have so much fun when I'm doing it, I'm sure it resonated. After about 30 minutes, a man who was juggling in the park came by and started juggling near me and we just smiled at each other and kept on doing our thing. As people started coming by, they thought we were an entertainment act and started putting money on the ground. I didn't make much that afternoon but I did make enough to buy a coconut water in a real coconut!

Exercise Routines

I've trained for ultra-endurance races through some of my heaviest business travel times. When I competed in Ironman triathlon, I was training 15-22 hours a week. No one *needs* to exercise that much but if you think you don't have ten minutes to exercise than I'll play the world's smallest violin for you.

The most important thing is to have a routine. I am a morning exerciser but most of the time I do something twice a day. The second session may be more of an activity than a workout but I do *something*. Morning exercisers tend to be more consistent for the obvious reasons: no excuses i.e. working late, plane delays, or too tired from traveling; the cue is always the same 'I wake up, I exercise'. It sets the pace for your day and unlike intense evening exercise, it doesn't disrupt your sleep. I have a challenge with Lift.do called the **10 by 10** to exercise 10 minutes by 10am as a healthy, lifelong habit.

Not a morning person? Give yourself ten minutes. You can wake up ten minutes earlier and do something, anything, to get your heart rate up and get moving. The metabolism boosting effects can last up to an hour. Do that a few times a day and you have given yourself little boosts that will not only make a big difference for your day, but a huge impact over the course of a lifetime. If you are *only* doing short bursts, some of these should be high-intensity bursts where you are breathing heavy and really getting your heart rate up. If you are able to exercise for 40-60 minutes, you can fit in an easier ten-minute burst 1-2 more times throughout the day.

Clothes and accessories

As far as clothes or other accessories to make your life easier, I always take wicking apparel. This helps the sweat to evaporate so if you are lucky and you have a little bit of time, your clothes can dry out a bit before you pack them. I always throw them over the air conditioning vent while I shower and stuff newspapers (The USA Today sports section is appropriate) in my sneakers to help soak up some of the sweat. The sneakers I use are low profile, which is more towards the 'minimal' genre. These are shoes like Altras, Vibrams, Nike Free and New Balance Minimus. They pack lighter and take up much less space than your traditional sneakers. I also keep spare headphones in my bag at all times so I don't forget them. I can't stand running on a treadmill without watching TV or listening to music. For safety purposes, you should use a Road ID whether you are exercising indoors or outdoors. They come as bracelets, sneaker tags and dog tags. I have a bracelet with my name, emergency phone number, doctor's name and number and health information. If you are someone who has a pacemaker or a diabetic who requires insulin, this could be very important if something were to happen to you. Something else I like to have is a **Sprigs Phone Banjee** wrist wallet. This is a great little travel companion. It will hold a smart phone in one pocket and your key card and credit card in a zipper pocket. It's made of wicking material so it can be washed and is super light. It's great to have in the fitness center but also to wear around an airport so you can pack your things away and only have accessible what is absolutely necessary!

Once when I was training for an Ironman, it was dark, cold and raining in Greenville, SC. I had to get a 20-mile run in and start at 4:30am to achieve it before work. I did this on a treadmill in a room with no television. This was before iPhones when all I had was an iPod shuffle. I forgot my headphones. How I made it through, I'll still never know.

Sleep on the Road

How many of you have laid in bed in a hotel listening to your neighbor's television, snoring or toilet flush all night? I used to be chronically tired until I started incorporating a few sleep hacks. First, I travel with an eye mask. I need darkness when I sleep. The light from the curtains that never seem to close all the way, coupled with the light coming in from the door to the hallway is enough to bother me. I have a cheap little eye mask I use and someday I may splurge on a nice silk one. I keep a large binder clip in my bag to pull the curtains all the way shut so that little bit of light doesn't peek through.

Custom-made earplugs are inexpensive or you can use a white noise app. I use this hack all the time to drown out distracting noise, not just when I'm sleeping. The specific apps I use are Sleep Machine Lite and Calm. They are free and you can get sounds like rain or white noise and have a timer so it won't drain your battery. I usually sleep with my phone in airplane mode and my app easily lasts all night with juice still left in the morning. There is also a YouTube video called *12 hours of white noise*. I'll put this on my laptop in the hotel room and then open the lid just enough that it stays on. At home I use the Ecotone Sound+Sleep Machine. It's a little pricey but the sound adjusts as the noise in the room gets louder. We live near enough to a doggie day care that we can hear the dogs bark all night long even with the windows closed. After getting this machine, we sleep soundly with no woofing serenades.

One night my phone rang when I was sound asleep in the hotel. I answered and no one was there so I assumed it was my wake-up call. I got up and turned on CNN and did a full warm-up in my room with my SMRT-Core. I was so tired I couldn't believe it. I dragged myself to the fitness center thinking I must be sick because I was feeling so bad and the start of my run was awful. I kept flipping through the channels on the treadmill TV wondering why it was nothing but infomercials. After about a mile I decided to settle on CNN Headline News and saw the time was 2:45am! I looked at the fitness center clock – 2:45am. Evidently, my call had probably been a wrong number and I was too out of it to question it. I promptly got off the treadmill, rinsed off in the shower and crawled into bed to sleep another three hours. It was the last time I used a wake-up call so now I know if the phone rings, it doesn't mean I have to get up!

Do you wake up in the middle of the night and have trouble getting back to sleep? Many times this is due to a drop in blood sugar. I always make sure I have some kind of snack like nuts, fruit or a minimally processed bar handy when I am in a hotel in case I need it. Since my meals aren't always perfect on the road I have sometimes gone to bed without taking in enough calories. On the other hand, if you take in too many calories or a lot of sugar or caffeine you may wake up often due to the highs and lows of the effects of the stimulants. At home, I started making something called 'Marcey's Concoction every night before bed. It consists of .5 scoop of Vega protein powder, 1T of unsweetened shredded coconut, .5 T of chia seeds and 1T of natural almond or peanut butter mixed with a little bit of hot water until it is a pudding. It is the perfect amount of calories, protein and fat to help me get past the blood sugar drop halfway through the night and keeps me from waking up. I travel with all three sometimes so I can just make it in my room.

One thing I would NOT take is prescription sleep aids. The research that has come out related to the effects of prescription sleep aids is astounding and having worked in the pharmaceutical industry for a decade, I know it does not take a significant benefit to get a drug on the market, ex. falling asleep 15 minutes faster with medication. Prescription sleep aids have been linked to memory impairment, loss of balance, morning hangover, dizziness, sleep walking, sleep eating, sleep sex (as in, not remembering that you had it!), depression, headache, dry mouth and constipation. I could go on and on. I'm not anti-drug for everything and I used to actually take sleep aids but when more research came out I stopped them immediately.

Always check the hotel alarm clock. I learned this the hard way when I was awakened at 3:45am one morning. Make sure it is turned off.

Light show

Forty-three percent of polled adults say they rarely or never get a good nights sleep and 95% of those used a computer or phone within the hour before bed. In order to get to sleep easier, it is very important that you don't stay on your computer or smart phone until right before you turn out the light. Your brain needs time to wind down. Studies have shown that the bright light of a computer screen may suppress melatonin and affect body temperature and heart rate. This has much bigger implications than just sleeplessness. Melatonin suppression has been linked to increased risk of cancer, type 2 diabetes, metabolic syndrome, obesity and heart disease, as well as impaired immune function.

Blue light is the most melatonin-suppressive and is emitted by TVs, computer screens and phones. Blocking blue light has been shown to be very effective in reducing melatonin-suppressing effects. I try to shut my computer down an hour before bed and also try not to look at my iPhone too long, maybe just quick peeks at my calendar or the weather for the next day. I have a Kindle Paperwhite to read at night specifically because I don't want to use the screen and mess with my brain waves.

While you're weaning yourself off of the computer or phone before bed, there are options you can try. I downloaded an app on my Mac called f.lux. It's free software that warms up your computer display at night and adapts the to the time of day. Blue blocker glasses can also be helpful and they are very inexpensive. Keep one set in your luggage and another set at home. Even regular light in your house can suppress melatonin so if you really have issues with sleep, it's worth putting them on when the sun goes down. Embarrassed about wearing glasses at night? In a hotel room no one will see you. At home, still probably no one will see you except your spouse or your mates (and they shouldn't care). Weigh the pros and cons – better sleep vs. feeling a little silly? I vote for better sleep.

Besides the fact that the light plays with your brain, do you really want to get an email late that will upset you or tell you about a new task or project you are assigned to? You don't have time to do it, yet now it is on your mind and probably disruptive to your sleep. Don't bother looking at it.

Avoiding Illness

Unless you live in a bubble, it is impossible to avoid *ever* being sick, but paying special attention to some of the things listed in this book will certainly help in prevention. Hotel cleaning staff are typically overworked and underpaid and most hotel rooms are not cleaned as well as you think. In order to keep from picking up someone else's germs or virus, I recommend paying special attention to the key things listed in this chapter.

I carry cleaning wipes with me in a sealed storage bag and wipe down my room when I get to the hotel. I wipe down the bathroom faucet handles, all of the door handles and light switches, toilet seat and handle as well as the desk, nightstand and remote control.

The bedspread may only get cleaned once every couple of weeks. I usually take it off of my bed immediately. If you are a member of the hotel honors program, you can usually request in the settings to have your comforter removed before you get to the room.

I recommend wearing socks or slippers on the carpet at all times. I use one of the big bath towels as an exercise mat so I don't have to get face to face with the floor. Carpets don't normally get swept between each guest.

The coffee maker may get a rinse out but rarely is washed. I would wash it out in the sink if I were going to use it. I usually get my hot water from the lobby coffee maker, as I would hope this gets cleaned more often since it is in sight. One hotel insider website states that they have found vomit, urine and cigarette butts in the coffee makers. Yummy!

Never drink out of the glassware or coffee mugs! Sometimes these just get wiped down with whatever rag is being used to clean the rest of the room. Only drink out of the disposable cups or use your own. Also, never use the stir sticks unless they are in packaging. Who knows where that thing has been or who has touched it!

The towels aren't always changed if it looks like they haven't been used. A former colleague of mine stated that she throws all of the towels on the floor before she leaves so they will wash them for the next guest. I reuse my towels just like I would at home if I am going to be staying there for a few days. I typically end up using all the towels because I use one as an exercise mat and put another on the desk chair. I don't have cleaning staff come to my room that often, so by the end of my stay, most of my towels are used anyway.

I wouldn't use the ice bucket unless it has a plastic liner with it. Have you ever seen hotel staff switching out ice buckets? That's because they don't get cleaned! Don't assume people are only storing ice in there either. I know someone who routinely uses it to soak her feet (and I've seen her feet!).

The remote control is the absolute dirtiest thing in the hotel. You can clean it with a wet wipe or simply stick it inside of a bag or shower cap so you are only touching it through the plastic.

I don't often swim in hotel pools. The CDC found that 16,569 hotel/motel pools had the highest rate of closure due to serious code violations. This is about 1 in every 6 hotels. They are pools of fecal matter, urine, shigella and norovirus. Most hotel pools are heated which is why these bacteria and viruses thrive. If hotel pools are bad, imagine what the hot tubs are like? Giant petri dishes waiting for you to sit in them and take up residency in your body. Neither pools nor hot tubs get cleaned regularly in hotels.

If a fitness center has wipes, use them! If they don't, tell them at the desk that they should get some. When I have the time to fill out the hotel questionnaires, I always request this if they don't have them already. I was so happy when they started having these available. If they don't, always use a towel and try to avoid touching your face while you are working out. Fitness centers basically get a cursory wipe by hotel staff and are rarely disinfected.

Don't Let the Bed Bugs Bite!

Bed Bugs are a hot topic right now and for good reason. Hotels seem to be infested with them and if you bring them home, it is extremely expensive and inconvenient to get rid of them. It doesn't matter how luxurious the hotel is since they have even showed up at the Ritz-Carlton. You can go to bedbugs.com, but by the time it is listed, the hotel may have taken care of it. They may be the cleanest of all because they are hyper-aware and probably fumigating more often. Bed Bugs can hop from luggage to luggage in overhead bins or be hanging out in the trunk of your rental car waiting to hitch a ride. There are some things you can do to help prevent them but there is nothing really foolproof to 100% guarantee you won't take them home.

1) Use a business card to run along the cracks and crevices around the mattress, bed frame or headboard to see if there are any bug remnants.

2) Travel with a small flashlight to inspect for fecal or blood matter.

3) If you see signs, alert the hotel immediately and move to another floor. Bed bugs travel up to 15 feet so moving to the next room is not an option.

4) Leave your clothes in your luggage away from the bed. Don't put them in the drawers. I keep my luggage in the bathroom if there is enough room or on top of the sink.

5) Fabric luggage is more attractive to bugs than hard-shelled luggage.

6) Travel with a large plastic bag. If you think you may have been exposed, encase your luggage.

7) When you get to your car at the airport, put your suitcase in a plastic bag prior to getting in your car.

8) Leave your luggage in a hot car or hot area, like a garage, for a couple of days. Just remember to pull out any toiletries or meltables.

9) Laundering your clothes in hot water or dry cleaning is recommended, however, unless I thought I had them, I wouldn't do this. I don't wash anything in hot water because most clothing doesn't react well to high heat and it takes a lot of energy.

10) Inspect suitcases before putting them away.

Not everyone reacts to bedbugs the same way. I had a client who had bed bugs and didn't react to their bites. Her sister came to stay with her and they slept in the same bed and she woke up with bites all over her. That was the only way she knew her home was infested.

Bed Bugs or not, for hygiene purposes, if you are afraid to sleep on the sheets, I recommend a silk sleep sack. I got mine at REI and it's lightweight and folds up next to nothing in your carry-on. I just crawl in it and then put the hotel sheets on top. If I'm in the sleep sack because I'm worried about creepy-crawlies, I stick it in a sealed, plastic bag before I put it in my luggage and throw it in the laundry when I get home. Even if the sheets are clean, the detergents and bleach they use are so strong that I've known people who have gotten rashes so the sleep sack helps with this too.

Hotel Safety

Hotels can be dangerous places, especially for women, but there are a number of ways you can protect yourself and be smart. When checking in, ask the hotel staff not to state your room number out loud. Preemptively, ask the staff to 'please just point to my room number and not say it out loud' to save you both the trouble and time. They should all know better than to do this but I still find desk staff that advertises it about half the time.

Always ask for two key cards at the hotel. First, it doesn't alert anyone around you that you are traveling by yourself. Second, you keep one card on your person in a pocket and another in your purse or bag. That way, if your purse or bag were to get stolen, you would still be able to get into your room. I take a photo of my hotel door so I remember the room number.

One trip I was in three cities in one week. On the third night, I checked into my hotel and went to the hotel gym to work out. I was sweaty and gross and tried my room key in my door. It didn't work. I went down to the desk and told them my key wasn't working. They said that the room number I had given them was not my room. I was mixing it up with another hotel I stayed in earlier in the week and could not remember what my current room number was! Since I didn't have my driver's license on me, they wouldn't tell me my room number. I offered several times for them to go with me into my room and get my license and they wouldn't do it.

At this point, I was seriously ticked off. It was obvious I had been working out and did not have my license with me. I was also a Platinum member at this chain and had stayed at two of their locations earlier in the week. I couldn't believe they considered it safer for me to walk the floors trying doors then to just follow me in to a room. That is what I did though. I walked up and down the halls of two floors before I finally found a door that worked! Lesson learned.

Be careful when going *into* your hotel room. If someone is in the hall with you, wait until they have passed by before opening your door. It is easy for someone to push their way in and trap you inside. Once inside, *shut* the door but don't lock it with the deadbolt yet. Before you use the deadbolt and bar, check the shower, behind the drapes, the closet and the sliding glass doors, to make sure that there isn't anyone waiting for you. Check to make sure the door is all the way latched when entering and exiting and use both the deadbolt and chain or bar. Once I got out of the shower to find housekeeping in my room when I didn't use the bar. Awkward.

One night I was dead asleep about 11:30pm and heard someone trying to get in to my room. I got up and looked out the peephole and there was a family of four looking tired and irritable. The door was able to open for them but thankfully it was latched with the bar. I told them the room was occupied and they needed to go back to the front desk. Well, this family must have been really exhausted because they started arguing with me that it was their room. I finally opened the door in my pajamas and said 'Look, I have been asleep for 2 hours so clearly this is my room. You need to go downstairs and get another room.' It was a mistake on the hotel's part and I let them hear about it in the morning. If the bar hadn't been across the door, they could have used the key to get in and at a minimum, woken my peaceful slumber.

Label your things, just like summer camp. I have a label on the outside of my suitcase as well as a business card on the inside in case the outer label gets ripped off. As much as I don't want to mar my beautiful MacAir, I have a label with my phone number on the bottom. When I had a less beautiful laptop, I just taped my business card directly on the bottom. I highly recommend this as well as putting your IT number on the bottom. If you can't get your computer to work, having your IT number saved in your *My Documents* isn't going to help you.

I have scanned my passport, driver's license and insurance card and stored it in the cloud so if something were to get stolen, I would be able to at least show a scanned copy in order to provide numbers or to help me replace them. I also have the phone numbers of my credit card companies stored in my phone so I can call ASAP if they are stolen.

Fire department ladders typically don't go above seven floors so consider staying on a lower floor, even though you may not get the best view. On the other hand, staying on a ground floor can open you up to theft easier. If you are staying at a hotel with rooms that open from the outside, try to stay near the office or some other semi-busy area. Try to avoid staying in a room that adjoins with another one (unless you know the person of course!). If you can't avoid it, put your luggage rack or the office chair in front of the door so you will hear it if someone tries to open it.

Do not prop your door open while you are getting ice or while you are waiting for room service. **Never** open your door to anyone without making sure that they are indeed hotel staff. When someone knocks on my door I ask their name and call down to the desk to see why they are there unless I am expecting them.

I use my *Do Not Disturb* sign the entire time I am in a hotel. Unless I am staying in the same room more than three days, I decline housekeeping. I'm not a dirty person, I don't clean my house every day at home and it keeps people from being in my stuff. If you hang out the sign that the room needs attending, it is a sign to thieves that you are not in the room. Many people also leave the radio or TV on. I have a hard time with this because I try to be energy efficient so sometimes I do and sometimes I don't. This is your call.

Always use the in-room hotel safe in your room for your jewelry, valuables, phone, extra cash, passport and laptop, even if only for a short time like a trip to breakfast or the fitness center. I test out the code and make sure it is working before I put my things in it to ensure something doesn't get locked in that I can't get out. Use a code you will remember like your house number, part of your zip code or your PIN. Don't use easy to remember codes like 1234 or 0000.

Step 3 – Auto

Road Trip Nutrition

Packing for a car trip is easier than air travel because you can take a small cooler. My husband and I drive eleven hours a couple of times a year and also take road trips on weekends for races. When I have work in my home city, I pack a cooler with snacks if I don't plan on eating out with a client. Some of my staples include:

- Hard-boiled eggs

- Edamame (just let it thaw naturally)

- Nuts

- Homemade trail mix

- Fruit

- Dried oats for oatmeal or muesli

- Homemade muffins

- Individual packets of nut butters

- Protein powder

- Baby carrots, peppers or celery sticks

- Hummus or bean dips

- Bread or tortillas

- Single serving Wholly Guacamole packs

Emergency Snack Attack

I keep single serving 100-calorie bags of nuts in my car at all times. This helps when I'm starving and on my way home. I can have a bag and then not make a bad decision by eating too much when I arrive. It's also good in an emergency. I have two friends who have each sat on a highway for more than three hours due to an accident. In the South, when there has been snow or ice, people have been stranded in their cars or taken 3-4 times as long to get home. If you were already hungry, imagine how you would feel after three hours! For someone with diabetes, it is even more important to keep some kind of snack in the car in case your blood sugar gets low. Dried fruit works well too. The key is to make sure they are things that won't melt or freeze.

Rental Cars

A lot of business travelers forget where they parked their rental car or even what kind of car they have. I don't know how many times I have picked up a car in the evening and not paid attention to the color, driven to my hotel and the next morning, wandered through the parking lot trying to figure out which car was mine. I have opened trunks or started the alarm to find it and when the car keys didn't have either option, I have even tried unlocking doors. Now I take a photo of it and where it is parked before I walk into the hotel.

A woman checked her car in with the valet and was given the wrong car the next morning. Because she didn't remember what car she was supposed to have, she was halfway through her day when she realized it wasn't her car. The poor woman whose car it was had left some of her things in it in the backseat. It was a panic for both of them but they were able to get it sorted out eventually. It's a good idea to keep your rental agreement with you in order to double-check your car the next day. It also is safer than leaving it on the seat, making it obvious that you aren't from the area. Alternatively, you can also leave something to identify it like an empty bottle, pen, anything that will alert you that it is your car when you get in the driver's seat the next day.

When I park my car at the airport I write the location on my ticket stub since I have to pay in the airport before I pick up my car. I sometimes take a photo of the location that I have parked at the airport too. There are apps that will locate your car via GPS but so far I have been ok just taking the photo and then deleting it when I am finished.

Have your itinerary and directions stored in your phone, GPS or printed out and with you at all times. You don't want to be fiddling around with it in a parking lot or driving around in circles late at night. Ideally, you have voice GPS so you can look at the road while being directed where to go. You also want to find out where your lights, wipers and door locks are as soon as you get into the vehicle.

My husband was driving down the road at night behind a woman with her lights off. He blinked his lights at her a couple of times hoping it would alert her but she didn't turn them on. When they got to a stoplight, he pulled up beside her and directed her to roll down her window. He told her that her lights weren't on. She looked around the console, shrugged and said 'It's a rental' like it was an excuse not to turn them on! Off she drove with no lights.

Most airports will escort you to your car. Hotels will too, which is another reason why it is good to have the number of the hotel handy on your phone so you can call as soon as you get there or even when you leave the airport to prepare them for when you will arrive.

If you are walking alone, do not be distracted by your cell phone. On the other hand, if you think you *are* being followed, pretending to be on your cell phone is recommended because your assailant may be worried that whoever you are talking to could call the police and there would be a witness, even if over the phone.

If a van is parked next to you it is easy to be pulled inside. If there is a van parked next to the driver's side door, consider entering from the passenger side.

Always put your laptop in the trunk *before* you leave your destination so that when you park, if you aren't taking it in with you, like to a restaurant, no one sees that you have one in your car.

Taxis

I don't particularly feel safe in taxis but I often can't avoid them. Some cities the cars are unmarked and so it feels risky before even getting in. Always ride with licensed taxi drivers only. Take a photo of their license, which is usually on the back of the seat and clearly visible to you. This is a good idea in case you leave something behind as well. Calling a taxi service and saying you left your book in a taxi in NYC is like telling Wrigley you dropped your red marble in a giant vat of Skittles.

It is helpful for the driver if you have the business card or exact address of the hotel. I was dropped off at the wrong Hotel Millennium in NYC once and it took me an hour to get to the correct one. Have a general idea of the direction you should be going and how long it takes. You can GPS the route on your phone to make sure the cab driver isn't taking you the longer route.

Step 4 – Mobile Office

Mobile can be traveling by car, train or plane but it doesn't have to be traveling far or overnight. Many mobile professionals spend time just traveling around their region or from meeting to meeting, i.e. realtors, sales, pharmaceutical reps. Step 4 will cover general mobile hacks and really dive in to mobile productivity.

Stress Reduction and Relaxation

For people who travel weekly, there isn't enough time for their stress levels to drop prior to their next trip. According to the CWT stress index, this increases their stress score by four points. Even when your trip is easy, the underlying anxiety of traveling can take its toll. Stressful events include:

- Lost baggage
- Delays
- Strange rental car (where are the lights and windshield wipers?)
- No Wi-Fi
- Hungry, which can turn into Hangry
- Navigation in a strange car in a strange city

The list could go on and most mobile professionals are by themselves so everything needs to be taken care of alone. The Five Ps – Proper Planning Prevents Poor Performance can play a big part in it. What can you *plan* to reduce stress?

1. Scheduling a flight at a time that is good for you (fly in the night before if you aren't a morning person).
2. Getting to the airport with plenty of time to get through security and to your gate.

69

3. Packing snacks. Low blood sugar can lead to feelings of stress and anxiety.

4. Wearing clothes, shoes and accessories that are easy to remove for security.

5. Packing noise-cancelling headphones.

6. Scheduling time for exercise.

7. Maintaining as much of your home routine as you can while on the road.

Exercise

Exercise is a MAJOR stress reliever and can also give you energy. If you do nothing else, do ten minutes of exercise every day that you travel. Get your heart rate up and get moving for 10 minutes. If you can't find 10 minutes in 1440 minutes per day, there are some serious excuses being made. Check out my challenge to exercise 10 minutes by 10am every day on **www.Lift.do**.

Meditation

One thing I think is happening to our society is that we feel we have to always be busy. We have forgotten how to just sit and be still or present. I am as guilty as anyone and feel like I should try to be productive everywhere, however sometimes taking that mental break is what makes me more productive. I installed an app on my smartphone from Calm.com and after several years of trying, have managed to meditate daily using guided meditations. What's great about Calm.com is that some of them are only two minutes long and there are different meditations for focus, anxiety, creativity, forgiveness, etc. If you feel less than stellar but are unable to sit in the moment for more than a few minutes, put on a two-minute meditation. It's two minutes out of 1440 but can make a world of difference. I also track my streak on Lift.do. Having a streak makes me want to continue every day. Maybe you decide that you will just close your eyes and be still during takeoff or for five minutes before you turn on your computer when you get to your room. Meditation is going to the gym for your mind. Benefits include:

- Lowered acute stress response

- Increased concentration of gray matter in the hippocampus of the brain which is subject to the stress release of cortisol

- Reduced concentration of C-reactive protein, which is associated with heart disease

- Decrease in active inflammation and increase in immune system

- Lower blood pressure

Oh, My Aching Feet

Traveling can result in aches and pains in places you never knew existed and it is tiring to boot. I would treat myself 1-2 times per month by saving up some of my per diem or just saving some spending money and getting bodywork done in whatever city I was in. Some cities that I went to regularly I scheduled routine appointments when I was in town. Massage, pedicures and foot reflexology will definitely help your posture, muscles and your aching, tired feet. If you don't have the money or the time for bodywork, you can still do some things for yourself in your hotel room.

I've been doing ice baths for years. It sounds like torture and it is for a couple of minutes but it is so good for your body and if done in the evening, helps you sleep at night due to the rapid drop in body temperature. Stop at a convenient store and get 1-2 bags of ice and put it in the tub with water up to your hips if you are sitting. I don't do it Tim Ferris style and fill the whole tub, but I find that the ice baths really help for aching legs and feet! The research is proving positive effects are mixed but there isn't anything saying it's bad for you. I have used the hotel ice machine a few times but it takes so many trips it is easier just to go to a gas station and get a bag of ice to take back to the room.

Trigger Point Therapy or Self-Myofascial Release

I travel with a tennis ball and Trigger Point Therapy products. I have used them for about eight years and I think it is the key to my long career of training and racing. Self-Myofascial Release is performed with a foam roller or with TP Therapy products, which are far superior. For travel purposes, the TP Therapy Quadballer, Footballer and Massage Ball travel much better than a traditional foam roller because they are more compact. They will also last much longer and won't break down like a foam roller. If you aren't ready to make the purchase of a TP Therapy kit, using a tennis ball can work on some areas too. Self-Myofascial Release (SMR) can improve flexibility, muscle recovery, and movement efficiency, inhibit overactive muscles, correct muscle imbalances and reduce pain.

The most basic way to describe SMR is to slowly roll until a tender spot is found and then hold on that spot for 30 seconds. Then gently roll it out an inch or two at a time. This is great to do while watching a movie or listening to a podcast. At first, it might be uncomfortable, some will even say painful. I may have even heard the term 'torture' used a few times. This is one area where *no pain no gain* is true. If you have pain, then it is a jumbled up mess underneath that skin and you NEED to perform SMR. I highly recommend enlisting the help of a Certified Personal Trainer first to teach you how to correctly foam roll. If I could only enlist one product or supplemental activity I would use SMR and the TP Therapy system, hands down. If I could only buy one item, I would buy their SMRT-Core Grid Foam Roller. I encourage all of my clients to buy one. I also have the Performance Knee Kit but stopped traveling by air with it. I always had to have my baggage checked because the inline skate-type wheels always looked suspicious!

If you can't stand the thought of an arctic bath and don't want to spend money on any products, you can always lie with your feet or legs elevated against the wall. Not only is this a restorative pose, it helps with swelling from flying on the plane.

Routine

Routine helps in the prevention of stress. I used to be a corporate trainer and trained new business travelers. I would tell them if they were in a cool city to make sure they gave themselves a little bit of time to explore. However, if you travel frequently, that can actually cause stress if you feel like you *have* to go explore or see the sights. *What? I'm in Chicago staying on the Magnificent Mile and I'm not going to leave my hotel? I'm a block from South Beach and I'm not going out to the ocean?* Don't feel pressured to see the sights when you are traveling for business if it is going to make you feel more behind and stressed by doing it. Sometimes the best thing you can do is to continue your normal routine. If you work out in the morning at home then continue to do that on the road. If you eat oatmeal for breakfast then eat oatmeal for breakfast. Go to bed around the same time. Remember, business travel is not vacation and it is more than a job. It is a lifestyle. Do what you feel comfortable doing.

Tipping

Tipping gives you good karma. If you are a business traveler you are getting your trip paid for and reimbursed for tips so don't be stingy. Don't be ridiculous either or your company may single you out. Service workers to include: Airport skycaps, shuttle drivers (especially if they handle your bags), taxi drivers, hotel housekeeping, room service (check to make sure it isn't already included), valets and the concierge. If you are paying for your trip yourself and you are watching your budget, avoid using valet parking if you can and opt out of housekeeping every day by putting out the *Do Not Disturb* sign.

How Much?

According to Lizzie Post of the Emily Post Institute, you don't tip on the tax at a restaurant because that's the part the government gets. I never thought of that before I read her take on it. It is customary to tip 15% for good service. For excellent service, tip 20% and tell the service person and their manager that the service was excellent. If the service is poor, according to Ms. Post, you should still tip 10% but inform the manager about the issue. After checking various websites, I gathered the following most common tipping amounts:

- Airport Shuttle Driver – $1-2 or $1 per bag

- Skycap - $1 per bag

- Bellhop - $1-2 per bag or $2 minimum if they are taking it to your room

- Hotel Housekeeper - $2-5 per night (the messier you are the higher you should tip). Tip daily if you use housekeeping daily because you may not have the same housekeeper every day. If you aren't using the service daily, tip something at the end of your stay.

- Parking Valet - $2-5 to bring the car to you. If the weather is bad, tip on the high end.

- Hotel Concierge - $5-20 depending on the level of service. No tip is necessary for asking simple directions or recommendations.

- Room Service – 15% of the bill or at least $2 (not required if gratuity is included)

- Waitstaff - 20% for excellent service, 15% (excl. tax) for good service, 10% for meh

- Wine Steward – 15% of the cost of the bottle

- Bartender – 15-20% of drink tab, .50 soft drink or $1 per alcoholic drink. Make sure you always tip your bartender if you get something before you head to your table.

- Food Delivery – 10% of bill (excl. tax), 15-20% if delivery is difficult due to weather or traffic or $2.00 minimum. Delivery charge doesn't always go to the driver so be sure to tip!

- Coatroom Attendant - $1 per coat

- Washroom Attendant - .50-$1. I have to say, I seriously dislike the thought of washroom attendants. It makes me very uncomfortable to have someone in the bathroom handing me a paper towel. I know it is employment, but it still gives me the weirds.

- Taxi Driver – 15% + $1 per bag

Mobile Productivity

Have you ever made yourself busier than you need to be and somehow got satisfaction out of saying how busy you were? Why do people do this? We should want to be productive so we can spend our time enjoying our life and playing more. Right?

What we used to think of as hacks – faxing instead of mailing, emailing instead of faxing are now the conventional methods and we have become so inefficient at it that we have become consumed and even offensive in how we use it. Carlson Wagonlit Travel (CWT) determined that on an average domestic trip, travelers lose 6.9 hours per trip of productive time. The financial equivalent is approximately $662.00 per trip. This can't all be eliminated, but they have determined that companies could potentially control about 32% of lost time.

The highest triggers of stress are what they deem *surprises*: flight delays and lost luggage (the latter more stressful for women than men). Flying economy class was considered stressful due to lost productivity time. This was higher for men than women, because, in general, men are bigger or taller and it is harder to work crammed into a seat so they may not be able to pull out their laptops. Women also tend to experience four points higher on the stress scale overall than men. The most significant stressors for women were lost luggage, hotel stay, increased workload and weekend travel.

Attention Distraction Disease
(I made this up - not to be confused with a diagnosed case of Attention Deficit Disorder)

Before we get into hacks, it's important to understand why we do the things we do, even when they are self-defeating. Human brains have two kinds of attention: involuntary and voluntary. *Involuntary attention* is triggered by outside stimuli and is used for survival. It's important if you're trying to run from an avalanche, but our brains have a hard time determining that the phone ringing, pinging or buzzing isn't an avalanche and takes our brain out of focus mode. Almost ALL individuals have a hard time ignoring loud noises and flashing lights. This can be dogs barking, airplane noise or an iPhone ringing in the background.

Voluntary attention is the ability to focus on a task like writing this book or for you to read this book. How many of you have put this book down three times in the last 15 minutes to check something on the computer, get something to drink or answer the phone? Focused attention takes mental energy. It's working out for your brain. You may run an extra five minutes or complete a few more reps when you are training your body but no one considers training their mind. Forcing yourself to wait five more minutes before you check email AGAIN or committing to working for 30 minutes straight on a project or task is a workout for your brain.

*"Developing greater control over your attention is perhaps the **single** most powerful way to reshape your brain and thus your mind. You can train and strengthen your attention just like any other mental ability." Buddha's Brain*

As we constantly undergo interruptions, a part of the brain that regulates attention, *effortful control*, declines. The more you check your messages, the more you feel the need to check them. It is *truly* an addiction or compulsion and can take a long time to get over, because it is *actually a process within your brain.*

Multitasking Myth

It's probably obvious when we are multitasking we are not absorbing as much information as if we were really focused but yet we still do it. Whatever is learned while multitasking is less retrievable by the brain. Tasks requiring more attention like complex exercises are more adversely affected by multitasking during the learning process.

Procedural memory is how you ride a bike or tie your shoes. *Declarative memory* is remembering what you had for dinner last night or your friend's phone number. The part of the brain called the hippocampus manages demanding cognitive tasks and creates long-term memories. It is key for declarative memory. When you are multitasking or distracted, the hippocampus kicks the job down to the striatum, which handles mundane tasks. The striatum is the part of the brain that is damaged by diseases like Parkinson's where people have trouble learning new motor skills but no problem remembering things from their past. Sometimes, the mundane part of your brain is the one replying to the question on the conference call or writing a response in an email because that part of the brain cannot do two things at once. The striatum is the brain's autopilot. Do you really want your autopilot to send your client an email?

"Please review the deli for our monthly meeting."

This is an example of an email requesting review of an agenda that I wrote to my manager while I was talking on the phone. My friend was saying to meet her at Jason's Deli for lunch and I wrote this in my email. Thankfully I caught it before I sent it.

Statistics

Multitasking is not a behavior of a 'super-worker'. It's a sign of distraction and science agrees. If a person is trying to read an email while talking on the phone, the brain is trying to perform language tasks that have to go through the same cognitive channel. His brain has to go back and forth between tasks, therefore slowing it down. Researchers at the University of Michigan found that productivity dropped as much as *40 percent* when subjects tried to do two or more things at once. One of the study's authors asserts that quality work and multitasking are actually *incompatible.*

In a study at the University of Minnesota, test workers who switch-tasked or multi-tasked took **3 to 27** percent more time to complete the reading, counting or math problems. The harder the interrupted task, the harder it was to get back on track. This is in agreement with a Microsoft study from the University of Illinois that found it takes the typical worker fifteen minutes to refocus on a serious mental task after an interruption such as responding to incoming email or Instant Messages. It was also easier for them to stray and browse personal websites after the interruption. A study at UC Irvine actually showed twenty-five minutes!

According to the book, Rapt, to truly learn something your brain has to be focused 100%.

A popular interview question is *"how is your ability to multitask?"*. I had a trainee tell me they lied during an interview and said it was *'great'* but in reality, they knew that multitasking decreased productivity and they tried to avoid it. They actually thought twice about taking the job at that company after knowing that it was so important that it was an interview question!

Multitasking in the workplace has reached epidemic proportions. A study by the Institute for the Future reported that the average employee sends and receives **178** messages a day and is interrupted an average of at least three times an hour. The estimated loss of productivity by multitaskers to the US economy is **$650** billion a year. A study by the McKinsey Global Institute estimated that employees spend 13 hours a week or about 650 hours a year on email.

Definitions of Tasking

These definitions come from Dave Crenshaw's book, *The Myth of Multitasking: How "Doing It All" Gets Nothing Done*.

Multitasking

As people learn more about the decreased productivity contributed to multi-tasking, we can only hope it becomes more culturally *unacceptable* behavior. This is the hardest for me to stop; especially when I am doing something I don't like doing. I'm not suggesting that no multitasking should ever be done, but remember that if you are truly trying to learn something, you need to have 100% attention.

Background Tasking

Examples of background tasking would be watching TV while exercising or listening to the radio while driving. Keep in mind that not all types of tasking are bad. Studies have shown that certain types of music can make people exercise harder. Personally I catch up on podcasts while I'm cooking and cleaning. Maybe you scan documents while a video is loading. Background tasking can actually be efficient. My point here is to understand when it is beneficial, when it isn't and the different types.

Hypertasking

Hypertasking is when multitasking gets carried over into your personal life. This could be talking on the phone while driving (a very dangerous form of multitasking which is the equivalent to driving drunk!) or working on a laptop while drinking coffee and talking to a friend.

Switchtasking

Switchtasking is juggling two tasks by refocusing your

attention back and forth between them and losing time and progress in the switch. Switchtasking is a serious cultural problem. We are actually switchtasking more than we multitask because we are able to do it at such speed. We are under the illusion we are doing things simultaneously, but really, we aren't. If it is something that involves the same part of the brain, like writing an email and talking on the phone, you can't do them at the same time. The average person spends three minutes working on something before they switchtask. I have a friend that I talk to once every few months and I can always tell that she is reading email while she is on the phone with me. There is something about her tone and responses. She probably thinks she is an excellent switchtasker or multitasker but I'm on to her!

Now that we have some background on the statistics and research behind various levels of tasking, we can get started on working with some of our own issues surrounding tasking as well as look at other areas of productivity that are difficult to manage.

Email

What we all love and hate. It can make us happy, sad, confused, frustrated, laugh and cry. I can't think of anything as a society that we may now have such a love/hate relationship with.

OHIO. Only Handle It Once!

How many people have an inbox full of emails that they keep reading over and over and over again? Just like with paper documents, you should do your best to Only Handle It Once. If you see an email that is obvious by the subject line that you can't respond or react to right away, skip it! If you can't do anything at the moment, then waiting until you have the time to respond will give you more time to focus on your response or think about the content of the email. However, you can *process* it correctly to avoid rereading it 20 times or clicking through it on a daily basis. We'll go into that later.

The average person checks their email 36 times an hour.

Let's just say you check your email every 5 minutes. Then you are checking 12 times an hour, 8 hours a work day, 5 days a week, 50 weeks a year (assuming you aren't checking your e-mail while you're on vacation), which equals 24,000 times a year. If you work more than eight hours or check email in the evenings, it's even more!

If you're checking your e-mail 24,000 times a year, what are you sacrificing? What are you *not* working on during that time? Could you reduce your rate to every 15 minutes (a yearly total of 8,000) and be more productive with other aspects of your job? Just think about that number for a minute. You automatically reduced it by 16,000 times a year just by checking ten minutes less. Could you reduce it to once an hour or 2,000 times a year? Three times a day for 750? I have found three times a day works perfectly for me for work email and one time a day for personal email. In three years, I have yet to have someone hunt me down and say I did not answer an email in a timely manner. If answering an email within about three hours isn't timely enough, than the sender should be picking up the phone anyway.

I have made a habit of having five or less emails in my inbox every day when I am finished. This took me a few months to get down to but 90% of the time I have *zero* emails in my inbox. When I first got down to zero at my previous position I sent a screenshot to my former manager to prove it. That was what first made her realize that my work hacking had helped.

Remember, email is a non-urgent task. If something is truly urgent, you should be receiving a phone call. You teach people how to treat you. It only takes one time that they send an urgent email that you don't respond to in time for them to realize it was inappropriate to send it via email and they should have picked up the phone.

Have you ever sent an email late at night or early in the morning to prove what a hard worker you are? STOP. NOW. No one is impressed with that anymore and it is so easy to schedule emails to be sent at a certain time it doesn't even prove you were working that late anyway. Go to bed.

Email Processing

Processing email in batches by working offline can decrease incorrect or inappropriate responses and it just plain saves time. Processing email doesn't mean opening it, reading it, closing it and dealing with it later. Processing email means to start at the top or in some other systematic way and start going through the threads. Think about it this way...would you go out to your mailbox, open your mail and put stuff back in that you didn't want to handle and then the next day go back out to your mailbox, open the lid, open the mail and put back what you didn't want to handle again? This could go on for days and you wouldn't do that. You get the mail and bring it inside and hopefully, do something with it. It's like a conveyor belt. You have to do something with the chocolate as it comes by on the belt. Otherwise it will just pile up on the end. Maybe you package it, throw it away because it didn't pass quality control, move it to another belt that coats it in peanuts. Or maybe you even eat it, but you don't just let it get to the end of the belt and pile up because then the chocolates will eventually expire, melt or it will affect the worker on the peanut belt and now they can't do their job.

Email processing doesn't mean jumping around unless there is an urgent requirement that needs your attention. Remember, this is your focused email processing time! Schedule it just like anything else. Tell yourself 'I am going to process email for the next 25 minutes'. By telling yourself you are going to *process* emails rather than *respond* to emails helps to change the mindset because not every email requires you to respond. Many emails are for deleting, delegating or archiving. Read the email and either Delete, Delegate, Reply, Archive or create a Task.

The order of email processing can change. I would suggest if you are coming back from a vacation or more than a couple of days away, start with the newest first. Why? Because the older ones may already have worked themselves out and you don't want to waste any time working on something that is completed. Hopefully your email system is updated enough that all of your emails show up in threads.

Step 1. Start with your Delete and quickly scan to see which of your emails you can trash. These should be obvious...emails that missed spam, are outdated, forwards from friends/family/co-workers who send you junk, etc. The first few days you work on processing, instead of just deleting, go in and unsubscribe so you don't have to keep performing the same step over and over and over.

Step 2. Go through and see which ones you have to delegate so whoever needs it can start their task.

Step 3. Reply for those that you can reply to without needing to do extra work.

Step 4. Archive for the FYI type of emails. If you are only copied on an email and not in the 'to' box, it isn't your task and it isn't a priority. At least, that is how people *should* use the cc line.

Step 5. If the email requires research or action, create a new task in your to-do list. The point is to move it out of your inbox. Do NOT use the inbox as your to-do list. If you use Gmail and Google Tasks you can create a task directly from the email by going to *More* than *Add to Tasks.*

How do I start?

If this is your first time processing or you fell off the wagon and need to get back on, set a timer and give yourself 25 minutes to perform the steps above as quickly as possible. You will be amazed how fast you can go through them by following this order.

What if your inbox currently has 1000 emails? My recommendation is to simply create a folder and drag every single one of them except for what has come in the last week into that folder. If you are really brave and feeling frisky, just drag *everything but the current day.* Don't panic, they're still there and if they were important to you, you would have responded or done something with them, right? You can name this whatever you want – Archive, Irrelevant, it doesn't matter. Most of them are probably outdated and you don't need to do anything with them anyway. Start clean and work your way up from a week ago or even a day ago. Anything older is archived. Give yourself a fresh start. If you start with the old ones than the ones from today are already old by tomorrow. Start now. As Barbara Hemphill says, "*Clutter is Postponed Decisions™*" and that includes email.

Create rules or filters for emails that can skip your inbox but you need to refer back to. Examples of these could be: automatic notifications, confirmation receipts, or list serve digests. Even better, sign up for Unroll.Me. Unroll.me rolls up all your newsletters, digests and notifications into one simple email delivered morning, afternoon or evening. You can determine which emails you want rolled up and which ones you want to stay in your inbox. It is the #1 program I recommend to my clients. The only thing that bothers me about it is that it is free. It's too good. They could have made millions.

I used to dread going on vacation or even taking one day off because of the email overload. One thing to consider is that email is *another person's agenda* or task list. Think about that for a moment. No, really, think about it! Now, when you begin work, quickly scan for those things that are immediate or to make sure you don't have appointments you didn't know about and then **turn it off** for email processing time if you are able to work offline on your system. One thing to consider is the 'Four Weeks' folder. If there is an email with information you will only need for a short time, or you know you will need to refer back to it soon, drag it to a 'Four Weeks' folder. At the end of the month, go through and select all and delete the emails older than 30 days. These types of emails house things like webinar or meeting information that you might need next week but will be trashed after that. I use Gmail and Mailbox now so the search and boomerang capability is enough that I don't need to do this, but when I used to use Microsoft Outlook, I found it helpful.

Some processing may take thought and action and you only have so much time to process. You can have a folder marked *To Respond* and drag it there as long as you give yourself time at some point during the day to act. One thing I would refrain from is an auto reply that states when you read emails. This is just clutter in someone else's inbox and unless you won't be checking email for more than 24 hours, I don't think it is really necessary.

This email processing schedule and working offline was one of my first and also one of the hardest behavior modifications I had to go through. It's also one of the first things to fall off the wagon.

It's *so* easy with a smartphone to check email all the time, but what are you teaching people? You are teaching people you are always available. If you respond immediately to an email they will always expect immediate response and will start using email for urgent situations. Email is NEVER urgent. NEVER.

The way I made it through behavior change was starting with going online and downloading my emails every hour. Then I would work offline until I had Deleted, Delegated, Archived, Replied or Tasked. The anxiety was pretty intense at first. I felt like I was missing something and like I was doing something illegal or sneaky. My manager didn't realize I was down to checking email only four times per day until I had been doing it six months. She was so impressed that now, even though she hasn't been a manager to me for years, she will still send me updates to let me know her inbox is zero.

Trust me, when you start doing this, it will be perfectly normal for you to feel FOMO (Fear Of Missing Out), but once you realize that empires don't fall, people don't die and actually, your world and your business continue on, you will start to feel better and even a sense of satisfaction on what you can accomplish.

Subject lines

How can I become an email Ninja and decrease emails going back and forth to my inbox? Good subject lines are critical because they help to filter what is important, retrieve emails later and provide a timely response. Using a good subject line will help the recipient search for it and possible actions needed before they even open it.

Writing 'Action Requested' or AR and the date in the subject line lets a person know that they need to respond or do something by a certain date. When I put this in an email it tells the person that if they have more urgent needs they can get to my email later or that mine is a timely need and it needs to be prioritized. Writing NOT URGENT in the subject line tells the recipient that they can skip opening the email until they have more time.

One of my pet peeves is the subject line *Quick Question*. If it is quick, put the entire question in the subject line! If you can't put it in the subject line, than it is not a quick question. If it is just a one-liner, type it in the subject line followed by EOM, or End of Message. Then they don't have to open up the email.

No Thank You to Thank You

One big timewaster is the 'Thanks' emails. If someone goes above and beyond, for example, stays late from work in order to get a signature that I need, I will email back and thank them. However, if someone is just doing his or her regular job, I usually don't respond back. Why? Because it is an email that they have to open and delete. When I used to be a manager I asked my staff not to respond with 'thanks' emails unless I did something above and beyond what I should be doing. Deleting 'thanks' emails is an extra step. If I didn't go out of my way to do whatever they were thanking me for, I wouldn't have even noticed if they didn't thank me! How many people would *actually* notice if someone *didn't* write back a 'thanks' email for routine things? I mean, who has gone to bed at night thinking *'Gee, I sent that letter to my manager to review and they didn't reply back and say 'thanks'?* Sometimes we don't even mean it. It is more just a confirmation that we received whatever they sent. If this will be hard for you, just consider if it is necessary. It may depend on to whom it is going. Some clients may need a 'thank you' but your spouse, sister or colleague may not.

No Email Fridays

Some companies have gone to *No Email Fridays*. It is a movement where no email can be sent on Friday or at a minimum, after 12:00 on Friday. This would be hard for many companies, but I'm sure people could call more and cut back on emails on Friday. Do you know why this is a movement? People don't want the Friday Dump. In other words, receiving an email late in the day on Friday with a deliverable for Monday or anything that will make you shut down your computer and stress about it over the weekend is considered a 'dump'. Maybe it isn't realistic, but one thing to consider is if you would call a person and ask them to do something at whatever time you are sending the email. For example, would you call someone on Friday at 6pm or Saturday at 10am and ask him or her to create a new presentation for you? Probably not, but emailing it now seems culturally acceptable. I think saving that email until the workweek is much more appropriate and lets people enjoy their weekend. If **you** want to work that's fine, but you shouldn't expect others to work unless their job is to work on weekends. Save it in your drafts or schedule it to send on Monday.

Folder-Less or Folder-Free?

Stop making folders for everything! With most current email systems like the newer versions of Outlook or Gmail, the search capability is so extraordinary that if you archive something it is super quick to search for it. By searching instead, you have just removed the act of determining which folder it could go in (the receipt from your annual renewal for ACME Organization could go in *Receipts* or *Acme*), dragging it to a folder and then searching within that folder.

I only have a few folders because I filter or use my search function. If I'm looking for an email I type the subject and/or the person who sent it and any emails related to that search criteria pop up. I apply labels or filters that if a message from a specific email address arrives, it automatically gets sent to a certain folder after I open it or before I open it depending on what the filter rule is. It saves a step from opening and dragging or even opening if it isn't an email I actually need to read or is more of an FYI.

I admit this was hard for me at first. A place for everything and everything in its place. Now I just have a few folders like 'Travel' that I drag or label my travel docs to fall in to since I can't always remember what hotel I'm staying in to do the search. I have an Opt-In that all my opt-in emails go to when people sign up on my site. When I get one of those emails, it bypasses my inbox altogether and goes straight to the folder. I check this once a week and that is plenty.

Canned Responses and Templates

If you write the same email more than five times, stop rewriting and start using an email template if you use Outlook or use a Canned Response if you use Gmail. Installing a program like Yesware or Streak allows you to create templates or snippets.

Fact: the longer the email the less likely the recipient will read it.

Fact: the longer the email, the longer the recipient will feel the need to respond (if they respond).

Five Sentences

There is a movement called Five Sentences to help people have a personal policy against long emails. There are also three sentences and two sentences movements. At the bottom of your signature line you can simply state *Why is this email five sentences or less?* and list the link http://www.five.sentenc.es. My signature line includes *"To respect your time and mine, most responses will be five sentences or less."*

If you are requiring an action by that person, be very clear and direct in your email. If something is easy to address the person will respond. The more complex it seems, the less likely you will get what you need, even if it is important. Cut out excessive details but **don't** cut out praise. If someone went above and beyond for you, let him or her know it! I'm not saying we should be completely cold-hearted and omit *"hi, how's it going'....* but at the same time, if there is no greeting in the email to me and it is someone I know closely, it certainly doesn't offend me and I don't even think twice about it. I also don't need greeted after the first email of the thread. Say what you need to say and move on.

Reverse Office Hours

If you work as a team where you are expected to answer emails immediately, one thing you could try is reverse office hours.

Every team member has scheduled time during the day where they are not online. Unless your job is to answer emails all day, i.e. customer service, I have not seen this on a job description. You need focused time to PERFORM and ACT.

Apps

One app I highly recommend if you have Gmail is the free app *Mailbox* that can be installed on an iPhone or iPad. They are working on other platforms as well besides Gmail so check to see if they have new offerings. This app lets you archive and delete easily but the beauty of it is that it also has a delay feature. If you want it later at 2pm to remind you of the call-in information for your 2:30 meeting or because that is when you are processing email, you can have it resent then. If it's a blog post you want to read for pleasure, you can delay it until the weekend or when you are on vacation. If you have travel plans booked, you can delay your itinerary until the day before you leave so it can pop up when you need it. It's so easy. It supports up to ten Gmail, Google Apps or iCloud accounts. I *love* it.

Gmail also has the *Boomerang* service, which can boomerang emails back to you at a specified time. It's free for 10 emails per month and then 4.99 per month for unlimited personal or 14.99 per month for professional accounts. There is also Boomerang for Microsoft Outlook, which is only $29.95 and completely worth it. *RightInbox* is free software that allows you to 'send now', 'send later' (and schedule when), and 'remind me'.

Badges, Banners and Pop-Ups

One of the first and easiest things you can do is disable any pop-ups, envelope, badges or banner notifications. This includes removing your computer, tablet and phone. Remember earlier how every time your concentration is distracted you lose 15-20 minutes? Well, with those annoyances on all day, you are basically never focusing 100%. Badges are the numbers that show up on your phone to remind you how behind you are on whatever it is you are being alerted to. Some badges may be important like texts and calls so those should stay on. Definitely turn off your social media, RSS feeds and mail badges. You do NOT need to see how many blog posts or tweets are waiting for you to look at 24 hours a day. Just looking at 70 RSS feed updates to read makes my guts ache. Even if it isn't a necessity to read them, it can subconsciously cause you anxiety. To turn off these badges, go in to your settings, notifications and turn off any badges you don't need to see immediately. I promise that you will make it through the day without knowing that someone liked your photo of your lunch ☺

I recommend turning off your Instant Message (IM) or Chat function for at least part of the day. My rule when I used to work for a company that used IM was to turn it off the first and last hour of each day. That way I wasn't interrupted during my first hour when I was trying to plan and start my day and also not caught with a last minute 'quick question' when I was trying to wrap things up.

Speaking of instant message, let's give a universal pass to spelling and grammar errors on instant message and text. The vast majority of the time, I know what you are trying to say so you don't need to cost me money or time by sending another text or IM correcting your spelling or grammar. If I make the mistake, please don't point it out to me. You have way too much time on your hands if you are going to be Officer of Corrections for IM and text.

Sharing Documents

It isn't efficient to send documents back and forth over email all the time. First, it clogs up the inbox. Second, you may not know who has the latest version of the document you are working on. Storing documents in the cloud allows access from any device at any time from anywhere. Storage is free up to a point and then you have to pay a minimal fee but it's worth it. Some people sign up using different email addresses to hack their storage but I find too many accounts confusing so I just bite the bullet and pay when I need to. Cloud storage saves space on your phone, computer or tablet and syncs your files through all your devices.

Many people are afraid of the cloud and are worried about security. Cloud storage is more secure than email. If you are worried that your document will just go 'poof' think about if your hard drive went 'poof'. How do you back up your hard drive? Isn't it better to have it on a server backed up by another server than just sitting on your hard drive at home? There are many different services, but I'll just go over the ones I like to use and am most familiar with.

I like to share files and notes using Dropbox, Evernote or Google Drive and tasks and ideas via WorkFlowy or Mind42. There are so many applications for sharing beyond just documents; contracts, client files, policies and procedures, project plans, inventory and task lists. You can upload family documents and share as well. I have a health care directive uploaded to the cloud with my sibling each having the link. Below is a brief comparison and what I use them for personally.

Dropbox gives you 2GB of free storage plus 500MB of extra space for every person you refer. You can also get Pro Dropbox and upgrade your storage. A negative for Dropbox is that it cannot be worked in via real time. You must download the files that are stored there. If you like to share files to your Facebook Group, you can do this directly from Facebook. Dropbox has a 2-step verification feature when logging in to your account through the web or link to a new device with a security code sent to your mobile phone. When using the app, you need to punch in a 4-digit passcode. Only Dropbox has this extra step for security at the time I am writing this. Note that only Dropbox can support Blackberry.

- I put large files and photos in Dropbox to share them with other people via a link I can send. Then they can just go to the link and download onto their own computer. I don't store working files there as much as I do finished products since every time I open I would need to download.

Google Drive is available for those with a Gmail account and starts with 5GB of storage with more available to purchase. It has an online document editor that works like Microsoft Office. It has capabilities for documents, spreadsheets, presentations and forms. It also integrates with Hello Sign, which allows signature of a document without printing it out. Drive also has a 2-step verification feature when logging in to your account through the web or link to a new device with a security code sent to your mobile phone or you can use the Google Authenticator App.

- I love this for real time work with other people because the changes are seen immediately. I am on the board of our Home Owner Association and if we all have our laptops, we can make changes and adjustments on our own Drive and the others see it immediately. Whoever creates the document can give the others edit or read only access. We can all see the version history as well as any comments people have added. So efficient.
- I use Google Forms on my website for my Health and Productivity Scorecard. When a potential client completes the form, it alerts me and I can go right in to Drive to see the responses in spreadsheet format. The downside is that some people can't open the .gdoc format easily if they don't have Google Drive. Unless you are sharing with someone that has Gmail, you may want to opt for something else. Until I can find an app or program that has everything I want to offer a personal training client, I will use Google Spreadsheets to create workout plans and combine it with a Personal Training program I use.

Evernote captures screen shots, web pages, ideas, notes, and emails...basically anything you can think of! You can record an audio file, snap a photo of a handwritten note or business card and upload it via your phone. The search mechanism is extraordinary. We took photos of my husband's music pieces and filed the hard copies in a cabinet. By tagging the photos with words like 'marimba', 'solo', 'ensemble' etc., he can do a search in Evernote for the pieces, glance through them and then go directly to the hard-copy file that we tagged them under. It works perfectly. The search even works with handwritten notes and you don't even have to have great penmanship! Evernote can also be shared by document, entire folders or by link if the recipient does not have Evernote. The Evernote Skitch App allows you to easily mark up a screenshot or document. Ways I use Evernote include:

- Scan certifications, passport, driver's license and any other important documents so I have them on hand if my wallet is stolen and I need to provide proof.
- Folder called eBook Library for free eBooks I download but don't have time to read yet. I know they will be in my library folder when I have spare time.
- Download manuals online for electronic devices or equipment.
- Save entire webpages of info that I want to review or look at.
- Mark up my webpages via Skitch to give to my web designer.
- Recipe folder for any recipe I find online or when I take a photo of a recipe from a magazine.
- Client folders with photos and ideas.
- Workout folder if I see a workout online that I want to try. Instead of bookmarking, I just use the browser extension to save it.

Workflowy is one of my favorite programs. It is very simple to use as a list-making program that is searchable by hashtags or optical character recognition. What I really like is that I can share entire categories or just one section of a list with someone else that way they aren't all up in my biz and seeing all my secrets.

Time Management

Calendar management can be extremely hard as a business traveler. Your schedule isn't always your own and is out of your control if you are flying and there are delays. On the other hand, I sometimes am at my most productive when I am traveling because I don't have the distractions of the office or household chores and I am up in the air with no access to Internet. I can't decide if having Wi-Fi on planes is a good thing or not!

First, I recommend taking 15 minutes and watching tutorials of whatever calendar you are using. I can almost guarantee that you are not maximizing the capabilities and are taking steps that are unnecessary.

Then, determine if the calendar you are using is working for you. Sometimes if it isn't, it is just because you don't know the shortcuts or how to use it correctly, thus watching the tutorials can help. Other people want to be electronic but their heart is really with paper and they feel outdated if they continue using it. Use what will work for **you**. There are streamlined electronic calendars and there are beautiful, functional paper calendars. It is all very individual.

Scheduling

A big issue people have is figuring out how much time to schedule for specific tasks or meetings. Think about how much time you are *actually* working on a project. Chances are, a lot less than you think. We tend to spend our time on things that can be done quickly and are menial instead of the things that are really important. I am guilty of this as well and have incorporated the Pomodoro Technique, which I'll discuss later.

One of the best things I have done for my schedule is to have one day every week as my GSD or Get Shit Done Day. I make sure I have one day each week where I don't leave my house or have very few meetings. I save my most intense work for this day, i.e. writing, creating content, working on client plans.

Meeting Planning

As a former manager I was instructed that I needed to have one-hour meetings with my direct reports at least every two weeks (and ideally, weekly) but the high achievers didn't really need this. Our meetings would last 15-30 minutes and really just quick check-ins. I didn't try to stretch it out just because it was on my calendar. Since all of them traveled it sometimes became a nuisance part of their day. It was much better when I just checked in when I needed to and they did the same.

Stop inviting people or accepting invitations to meetings unless it's really necessary for you to attend. If you aren't sure, ask the person how important it is for you to be there. Can you just read the minutes? Can you attend only part of the call and drop off when you are no longer needed? I'm sure everyone has been in a teleconference that lasted an hour but only five minutes was relevant. *Atlassian* states that an average of 31 hours are spent in unproductive meetings per month and 73% of people do other work during the meetings. When asked what the #1 timewaster was in the office, 47% stated meetings. If time equals money than we are seriously burning some cash.

Some companies are moving to standing meetings. When people have to stand in a room for a meeting, they go much faster. I like walking meetings if it is a meeting between 2-3 people, I don't have to take notes and it is a semi-quiet area. This doesn't mean power walking and getting sweaty. You can stroll along and talk. Getting out of your normal office environment can also improve creativity and encourage more openness in your conversation. Any runners out there will understand when I say that sometimes you are more forthcoming with information when you are running beside someone rather than looking directly at them. I would imagine it's the same with walking.

To get control of your calendar, take a look at it a month out and look at all the recurring meetings. Determine which ones are truly mandatory and if you are the person running them, see if they can be done less frequently or if they can be done in a shorter time frame.

Then, block out your calendar in the mornings before you want to 'arrive' and block out in the evenings when you want to go home or will be traveling. When you have a calendar that other people have access to, it is very important you keep it up to date. If you are traveling, that needs to be blocked out. I don't know how many times I tried to schedule meetings with people based on their availability in their calendars and they wrote back and said 'sorry, I'm flying at that time'. If you have shared calendars you're wasting other people's time by not keeping your calendar up to date.

Block out at least two hours in your day to perform your own tasks so you can have focused time. Ideally, this should be your best time of day to focus. In the corporate world, I had meetings almost every day that started at nine. This was unfortunate from a productivity perspective because it was right when I started my day and when I had the most energy to perform.

Scheduling Systems

There are many scheduling systems on the market that allow people to see open blocks on your schedule and request an appointment. I wish more people would look at my calendar and request a time instead of sending an email because it would eliminate at least three emails being sent, but for some reason, most people are still shy about requesting a time. Check out systems like Schedule Once (my preferred), TimeTrade or YouCanBookMe. Schedule Once allows me to block different lengths of meetings as well as syncs with my Google calendar so I never have to post availability. I also recommend using a Virtual Assistant for scheduling. I'll talk more about VAs later in the book.

Hi Jim,

It was great to meet you at the networking event on

Thursday. I would appreciate a quick chat on the phone to see how we might be able to help each other. Please send me your scheduling link or feel free to use mine http://meetme.so/MarceyRader to cut down on the email thread.

Apps

If you're someone who constantly checks their phone during meetings or repeatedly gets interrupted and you have an Android device, consider installing the Silent Time app. This allows you to turn your phone notifications off during scheduled meetings and set times of the day when you don't get calls or texts. It also allows you to set a group of people (partner, parents) that can still get through to you.

Task Management

We've already talked about moving your task list from your inbox. Some people use their calendar as their task list and if they are able to make this work for them then that's okay. I prefer not to have my task list on my calendar unless it is a recurring task at a specific time and I might need a reminder.

Making your inbox your to-do list doesn't work very well. It's hard to prioritize and there may be multiple tasks with multiple dates within one email. There is also the time wasted rereading that email or clicking over it 10 times a day. Instead, pull out the tasks within the email and put them in your task list or whatever works best for you. If you use Gmail, just assign to tasks in your menu bar.

If you are a paper person, there is absolutely no reason why you need to have an electronic task list. If paper works for you, stick with it. Something as simple as an index card every day that you write down your tasks can be gratifying to cross off and throw away when you are finished. I have a hybrid system where my quick thoughts go on a piece of paper beside me at my desk. Then if they need to go on my electronic list I put them there. What's great about an electronic list is I can have repeat tasks. For example, I write every day. If I check it off for today, it automatically moves forward to tomorrow because I have a rule that causes it to repeat. On Mondays I edit my newsletter so it's a recurring task.

Two apps that I like for tasking are Calengoo for iPad and GoTasks for iPhone. I like that GoTasks allows me to have different lists, assign dates and make recurring events. As a downside, if I remove any of my completed tasks it removes the completed tasks for all of my lists so it is something to note if you like to check/uncheck rather than make something recurring. There are a plethora of task apps out there. Pick the **simplest** one for you.

Top Three Tasks

I schedule my top three personal tasks for the week on Sunday mornings and my top three work tasks on Monday mornings. Either the night before or first thing in the morning, I consider my top three tasks of the day. Then I schedule according to my energy level or my appointments for the day. I try to abide by Brian Tracy's rule to Eat That Frog and do my most important or winner of Task Most Likely To Be Procrastinated but if I have a distraction at that time of day, I know I need to save it until later in the morning. If I know I am going to be working during a layover or while waiting for a client, I'll do things that I can quickly cross off my list without much focus. If it's writing or creating, I know I will need completely silent, non-distracted time and will wait until I am on the plane with no Wi-Fi (but headphones on) or in my hotel room. You can use the Eisenhower Method to consider prioritizing:

- Urgent and Important needs to be taken care of immediately. Either there is a crisis or you have procrastinated and it needs to be done NOW.

- Urgent but Not Important tasks are things that need to be done quickly and are associated with someone else. Tasks where other people are waiting for you to do something in order for them to work may be high priority so that you aren't the bottleneck.

- Not Urgent but Important help you move toward your

goals and should be scheduled appropriately, however if you procrastinate they can quickly move to Urgent and Important.

- Not Important or Urgent can be sent to the bottom of the list. These are things that are 'nice to have' or can be done during a light day or week. They are activities that are distractions and probably can be said "no" to.

Think of your tasks in terms of whether they are urgent or important. If they are both, then it should be obvious that is what you should work on, even if it means shutting down your email and completely focusing. If you know you have a flight in the evening and can work uninterrupted, postpone focus work until later when you know you will be able to maximize that time on the plane.

One question you should ask yourself is if the task is *value-added*? What impact will this have tomorrow, a month from now or six months from now? Will it actually make a difference in my business or to a client? Would they pay me for what I am doing or is it a 'nice to have'?

Reflect at the end of the day and try to see if there were any time wasters. What did you achieve? If you didn't achieve what you needed to, can you see where you might have been able to be more productive? For me, I can be more productive for certain tasks if I go to a coffee shop. Having people around me isn't as distracting as being in my home office with all of the things I could be doing around my house. Being at home with someone there is very distracting, which is why I save my focus work for when I am alone. Don't just focus on what you didn't get done though, look at what you **were** able to achieve and why.

Busywork

Stop being busy and start working! Busy isn't work. Busy isn't creating. Busy is waste. People become martyrs and braggarts about how busy they are and even I have fallen into this trap. I have had people take their voice down to a whisper to tell me they only work about 35-40 hours a week because they either feel guilty or they know that more work will get piled on them. It's too bad salaried people don't get incentivized for being efficient. One reason I didn't tell my former manager right away about how much time I was saving by processing email and working offline was because I was afraid I would just get more work added to my already full load.

The bottom line: If you can't decide which task should be first, think about which task will have the biggest impact on your day, your job or your life.

The Pomodoro Technique

I am a very distracted person so I learned to work in intervals. Maybe you work for 45 minutes and then give yourself 5-10 minutes of time to check your personal email or your social media. We are not robots. Everyone needs a break. At first, I felt guilty for taking these frequent breaks but then I realized I got so much more done because I was time capping and able to focus more. My brain wasn't so tired or distracted. You will undoubtedly take as much time as you give yourself, so cap it, focus and do it in less time.

Depending on what it is, I sometimes use the Pomodoro or Tomato Technique. The most basic way to describe it is to set a timer for 25 minutes and work completely focused on one thing. Then you get a five-minute break. It's best if this is getting up, moving a little bit and looking away from the computer. Then when the timer goes off, go through another 25 minute round. After 2-4 rounds, take a longer break of 15-20 minutes. If you think you won't get as much done, you're wrong. Unless you are someone who can get lost in your work or project (and I envy you) these intervals of short focus and short breaks will make you much more efficient. I was surprised to find that even 25 minutes is sometimes hard for me. When a thought enters my mind or I want to click on a new link, I jot it down on a piece of paper beside me and come back to it later. I also will put a tick mark on the paper every time I get distracted during that round. I realized after a few weeks what my good times of day were.

The Pomodoro Technique also helps to train you how long a project or task will take. Estimating how many Pomodoros to complete the email campaign and realizing it took me twice as long is helpful for planning my next campaign.

Concentration and Focus Programs

I use RescueTime which is a program installed on my computer that lets me block out distracting websites during my focus time. I can categorize websites, apps and programs from very distracting to very productive and see at the end of the day or week how productive I was. I have goals set and try to stay within those every day. RescueTime is free for the Basic Service but I pay for the premium.

Focus Booster is a timer app based on the Pomodoro Technique that runs in the background. When your 25 minutes is up it starts a 5-minute break countdown.

Concentrate allows you to create activities and allow only certain programs or sites to be allowed during certain times. For example, when I was working on writing this book, I blocked out everything. When I am working on my site, I allow Mailchimp and Hootsuite to be open.

Relate, Create, Research™

Depending on what kind of work you do, you may be able to incorporate something I call Relate, Create, Research™. Ask yourself the following questions:

Who do I need to Relate to today? Who do I need to contact or reach out to?

What do I need to Create? A presentation? A training plan? An email campaign?

What do I need to learn about? What information do I need to Research to perform my job or a task better?

I used to block time out daily for each of these tasks but now I try to block out entire days as I believe it allows me to focus better. At the time of the book I am going by the following schedule:

Mondays – work on website, newsletters and Relate

Tuesdays – GSD *Get Shit Done* Day where I try to have no meetings and just Create. Tuesdays are considered the most productive day, which is why I choose this day to work in the office and GSD. I also meet with my Virtual Assistant.

Wednesday – Relate, Toastmasters, face to face meetings, meeting with my accountability partner Melissa, errands

Thursday – Create, Research and catch up on blog posts, teleseminars, reading

Friday – Relate, Business Network International weekly meeting, 1:1s

Saturdays – Research and catch up on blog posts, teleseminars. No email.

Sunday – No work. No computer except for my weekly meeting with my husband going through the finances and calendar for the week.

Energy Scheduling

No one has the same level of energy all day long. Save the more mundane tasks like filing, timesheets, or expense reports for the time of day when you are tired. Did you know that there is a certain time of day when you should make decisions? In the morning your natural levels of serotonin are highest so you are going to make a more rational decision than later in the day or evening when they are lower. Decisions made in the afternoon are more likely to be made as the status quo, postponed or not decided at all.

If you don't get a good deep sleep your serotonin levels will be low and you are more likely to make decisions out of fear. Exercise is a precursor to serotonin so this can help in your decision-making. Moving your butt in the morning or at lunch can give you a boost mid-day or afternoon in order to fight off that decision postponement. It doesn't have to be a sweat session; even a 10-15 minute brisk walk can help. Eating a breakfast with high protein can also give you a boost a little later mid-day so your ability to make important decisions lasts a little longer.

Computer Clean- Up

I have a reminder on my computer for the first day of every month to do a clean sweep. I use *Easy Duplicate Finder* to help find and eliminate duplicates on my computer. I was amazed the first time I used it to see how many duplicate files and photos I had. I also get rid of all my .dmg files, downloads and any documents in my *Temporary* folder that are no longer needed. Your computer isn't infinite space. Clear up some of that hard drive and let your now speedy computer run more efficiently. If you do this regularly, like once per month, it saves time down the road. Clean out your trash while you are at it and remember that on a Mac, iPhoto has a separate trash bin so you have to empty both.

Passwords

Remembering a million passwords is difficult. A password program will save time and brainpower. Password programs like LastPass and Dashlane are recommended and have a free and premium feature. I used 1Password and was not impressed. It didn't always remember what I had saved previously and I felt like I was continually entering in passwords when it was supposed to be saving me time. Dashlane will remember your passwords, alert you when they aren't strong enough and will generate strong passwords for you. It also allows storage of credit cards so I don't have to pull out my credit card every time I need to purchase something online.

Apps

Unroll.me. I cannot say how much this program has saved me and helped in my quest for daily Inbox Zero. First, it shows you how many websites, newsletters and notifications you are subscribed to. Every time a new email comes in that you are subscribed to, it asks if you want it rolled up. Unroll.me rolls up all your subscriptions into one digest. Yep, one email at the end of the day or whenever you want to schedule it. This can include all your service updates, social notifications and newsletters. If you don't want them rolled up, you just leave it as is. I was shocked at how many different websites and subscriptions I had. Unroll.me makes it so easy to unsubscribe as well. I make it a habit to keep my subscriptions at no more than fifty. That sounds like a lot but when I roll up almost 75% of what I receive into my inbox, it really isn't. This might even be something that comes in twice a year, like my reminder from my dentist to schedule an appointment.

Of course you need good travel apps. I like *TripIt* and *iFly*. TripIt keeps track of your itineraries for car/plane and hotel. If you pay the yearly fee it will also keep track of all of your rewards points and miles. If you are a very frequent traveler it is worth it not to have to check five different airlines and four different hotels to see what your rewards status is. iFly will also keep track of your itinerary but can tell you what cafes, restaurants and amenities are in the terminal of the airport so it's really helpful if you are trying to plan what to do or eat during a layover. I discuss iFly more in the Health Hacks section.

How many times have you taken an exit only to find out that the gas station was four miles down the road? *Road Ninja* can help you map out your trip, tell you what gas stations, cafes, pharmacies and restaurants are at each exit and how far you will have to drive to get there. It even tells you gas prices! There are other categories too so be sure to check it out. Super helpful on road trips.

Weather Channel is easy to favorite and remove the city you are traveling to. Not only great for checking out the weather, but also for checking pollen levels (those in the southeast know this is a big one!). If you exercise outside, you will know when sunrise and sunset is so you can plan if you need to use that hotel treadmill. I also like Yahoo's weather app. It's very user friendly and doesn't bombard you with ads.

Say it and Mail It is great if you want to record a message to yourself or someone else. When you are done recording, you just click and mail it to the recipient or default it to yourself. I have had a thought while out running and without ever stopping, have pulled out my phone, recorded a message to myself and emailed it to myself to attend to when I got back. If you have an assistant, you can make them your default and when you have a thought, click send and it will go straight to them.

Lastly, I like *Find My Friends*. Some may feel this is a little 'big brother' but you can share your location only with chosen people and it is easy to turn on and off. When I travel I turn it on so my husband can see where I am. Not because he is cyber stalking me, but because I travel alone most of the time and if I were to fail to show up for an event or meeting it may not be apparent or alert anyone that something is wrong. At the very least, if someone called my husband to say "Marcey didn't show up for the meeting', he could see via GPS where I was. We have also used this when we were meeting somewhere because it can alert you when the person left and when they arrived (great for concerts!) It's easy to turn off if you don't want someone knowing where you are all the time. When I travel, I have nothing to hide from my husband and I feel better knowing that *someone* knows where the heck I am.

Social Media

Social Media can easily be a timesuck for people if they don't timecap or limit the number of days they check it. I used to have a personal page with less than 25 people because I felt like I could really only keep up with that amount of people the way I wanted to. I had certain rules so it was easy for me to explain why when someone asked to friend me, I had to refuse. I made a rule to only check on weekends and even then realized that I could quickly lose 30-60 minutes without noticing the time. Now that I have a business, I don't use it for personal at all and only use it for business-related matters and relationships.

I thought I would have FOMO – Fear Of Missing Out, but I don't find that I do. Yes, I miss some photos of friends but the research shows that it can actually lead to more negative emotions after using it; jealousy, social tension, isolation and depression. People are putting their best foot forward in social media so you aren't seeing the bumps in their roads. If social media overwhelms you and you are using it for personal only, I recommend deleting your old account and setting up a new one. I even used a fake name so I couldn't be found. Be pickier about who you friend and the businesses you Like. If they don't add any value than you shouldn't waste your eyeball's time in reading over them. My rules when I had a personal account were:

- Over 18
- No coworkers unless I hung out with them socially
- I would have them over to dinner if they were in town
- They didn't post inappropriately (I had to unfriend family members who do not know the meaning of privacy)
- Businesses or Pages had to be businesses or people I really supported and were interested in their product or service

Timecap Your Timesuck

Social media can be a huge timesuck. Before you know it you have five tabs open, three sets of photos, a video playing of a monkey on a pig and an hour has passed! I schedule 25 minutes a day of social media and that's it and I have a business! If you find that you get pulled in, set a timer. Life is for living, not tweeting.

Receipt Tracking

CWT's "Travel Stress Index" found that frequent fliers (30+ trips per year) get a high level of stress from lost time relating to the reimbursement of expenses. One statistic I found stated that business travelers spend approximately 2-3 hours per trip on the task of expenses and reimbursement. This should really take at least half the time.

Those of you who read my website or social media know I am a huge fan of Shoeboxed. This company has revolutionized receipt tracking. Most business travelers have a smart phone and the days of keeping your receipts and taping them to a sheet of paper to then scan and fax or email them to accounting should be over. With the Shoeboxed app for smartphones and iPads, you can simply snap a photo of your receipt, check if it is *reimbursable, deductible* or *I don't know* and submit. You have photo documentation of your receipt and when on the Shoeboxed website, you can see your receipt categorized just like it would be on a credit card. For example, if you went to the BP to get gas and snapped a photo of your receipt, you would see your receipt, *BP* and it would automagically be categorized into *Fuel*. You can even create your own categories. I keep my personal and business receipts in Shoeboxed and just check the box to categorize. It is so easy. If you have a lot of paper receipts, all you have to do is mail them in and Shoeboxed even gives you an envelope to do that. You can also just scan them using your desktop scanner. One part that I love is the browser extension so I can just clip and upload all of my electronic receipts that go to my inbox. For receipts that are emailed to me on a regular basis, I provide my Shoeboxed email address and it bypasses my Inbox and goes straight to m Shoeboxed account.

Their newest addition is a mileage tracker. For those of you that travel by car, you simply press start, it tracks your mileage until you stop it and it tells you how much you should be reimbursed. They also have a feature called Speedy Reimbursement so you can email the expense to be reimbursed directly from the app. A feature that is great for businesses is account sharing so your account can be shared with a bookkeeper, assistant or spouse. At any time you can run a report or import into financial software. The savings in time for you, accounting and your personal accountant will be invaluable! I had the opportunity to meet Shoeboxed at their headquarters for a user success profile and the people who work there are as great as their product and really stand behind what they do. They employ people from the TEACCH autism program to help with their scanning. I heart Shoeboxed enough that I became an Ambassador and did a teleseminar with them in 2014. Full disclaimer: If you use this link **www.shoeboxed.com/offer/marcey_rader** you'll get 20% off a business account and I'll get a little lovin' from them.

Financial

It's easy to stay up to date on your finances on the road. Besides Shoeboxed, you can use almost any financial software on your computer and as an app on your phone. For small business accounts, QuickBooks is robust and works well. For smaller, personal accounts, I like YNAB or You Need A Budget. I have used Quicken, Mint and Moneywell and prefer YNAB to all of them. They have great free tutorials and their customer support is fantastic. I actually still use YNAB for both mine and my husband's business account by setting up a separate budget in the program.

On a personal note, I don't use the time saving feature of automagically importing my statements. As soon as I make a purchase, or at least the day of the purchase, I enter the transaction into the mobile app or computer so I always know how much money I have. By entering it in manually, it makes me accountable and keeps my budget front and center in my mind. If I'm just letting the computer enter in everything, it's easy to overlook expenditures until it's too late and I've gone over my budget.

Paying bills and transferring money via bank apps or websites is pretty standard now and all your bills should be electronic. There are differing schools of thoughts on setting up to pay bills automagically or manually. It's a huge timesaver to have them paid directly by your bank but if you are the type who tends to overdraw your account or not pay attention to your statements, you should do it manually so as not to get surprised. I have most of mine on automagic bill pay but I still look at my statements. This is how I knew I was getting charged an extra $7 for a bogus Internet charge and $5 for a bogus phone charge.

File This Fetch is a program that fetches all of your financial statements and bills. Every time a new statement comes in it gets uploaded to Evernote, Dropbox or Google Drive (your choice). It has the highest security available in modern browsers and encrypts all the communication between File This Fetch and your accounts. I really like having all of my statements and bills in one place, especially during tax season.

Paperless or Less Paper?

Everyone dreams of having the paperless office. In reality, that is very hard to do. You *can* have a Less Paper office. Eighty percent of what people keep they never use and the *more* they keep, the *less* they use. Think about your papers and how often you rifle through them. Both my husband and I are self-employed and we have one two-drawer file cabinet that is enough to hold all of the physical paper we need. One of the drawers is mostly electronic peripherals and isn't even paper!

Most papers can be scanned and stored electronically via services like Dropbox, Google Drive or Evernote. When people say they are afraid to store things in the cloud on a giant server that is backed up by several other servers, I ask them if they back up their paper with more paper stored somewhere off-site from their office or house since a fire or flood would render them useless. Sometimes, the excuses are more just fear than logic. For more help or guidelines with paper, check out the book *Taming the Paper Tiger©* by Barbara Hemphill. I'm certified through her Productive Environment Institute.

Portable Scanners can save a lot of time and are super light now. They have great Optical Character Recognition so you can just do a keyword search after you have uploaded to your computer. The portable Doxie can scan directly to Google Drive, Evernote, Flickr and others. It only weighs 10.9 ounces so it can easily fit in your carry-on. NeatReceipts is another mobile scanner that weighs 10.6 ounces and uploads to the NeatCloud. Fujitsu ScanSnap weighs 12 ounces and has capabilities for scanning to PDF, editable Word or Excel file, business card scanning and the ability to upload Evernote, Google Drive, Salesforce, SugarSync or SharePoint. If you have a smartphone you can download DocScan and snap photos, organize into a folder and then email the documents. This way you can completely bypass the old scan and fax method.

Faxing and Electronic Signatures.

When someone asks me to fax something I wonder if they still have a rotary phone. A fax machine is about as 1980s as one can get minus the jelly shoes and neon pink. It also requires each person to physically be somewhere to get the document and risks other people seeing that document. Eliminate the paper by using an eFax service. I like Hello Fax. I can send and receive faxes as well as sign documents using the partner service, Hello Sign. I send all of my waivers and contracts this way to avoid the Paper Tiger.

SwiftFile

If you use paper files, I highly recommend a tickler file system, called the SwiftFile. It is a mobile filing system to remind you of bills, birthdays, invitations and appointments as well as to hold your specific paper documents for the exact day you need them. It has 31 unique folders for the day of the month and twelve taller month folders. If I had kids, this would be a necessity for me! After purchase, you can watch tutorials on how to maximize use.

Contacts

Customer Relationship Management (CRM) helps manage customer relationships in an organized way by database or marketing campaign and can track customers or campaigns over multiple channels such as email, search, social media and direct mail. For some smaller businesses and solopreneurs, it may just be a simple contact manager system that integrates emails, documents and scheduling.

Scrubly is a program that cleans up your address book by removing duplicates and merging matching contacts. It works with Outlook, Mac and Gmail. It can also add social data. I have two Gmail accounts and it looks through both of them to find similar names and asks if I wish to merge them.

I love *Rapportive*. This program can be customized with Gmail, Klout, Crunchbase, GitHub, MailChimp, Aweber and more. I have Rapportive installed in my Gmail so every time I am sending an email, it gives me information on the right hand side of my screen that includes the recipient's profile photo, LinkedIn profile, Location (if they have this enabled), latest Facebook, Google+ and Twitter posts and a spot for me to write a note if I need to. I love being able to learn more about people and instantly see their photo.

SendOut Cards is a wonderful tool to use for customer relationships and is super convenient when on the road. You can send cards right from your computer. The cost is cheaper than buying one from the drugstore, customizable with your own photos and you can schedule entire campaigns around marketing efforts or holidays. They also have an online gift catalog and gift cards to choose from. I use them to show before and after photos when I organize someone's office or desk or when they start a fitness program with me. People like getting personalized cards and having their photo on it will keep them from chucking it into the trash so it is more of a long-term advertisement.

Virtual Assistants

Write down everything you do and then look carefully at that list. If you consider what your time costs per hour, how much money are you wasting doing tasks you shouldn't be? Are you doing $10.00 an hour tasks? $50.00 an hour tasks or $100.00 an hour tasks? My guess is you are doing a lot of $10.00/hr tasks. Why? Because they are usually quicker tasks like scheduling, social media posts, researching flights etc. STOP. This took me some time to get used to but then I realized that I was spending a lot of my time doing $10 or $20 per hour tasks instead of working on my business. Enter the world of virtual assistants.

Virtual Assistants can do everything from scheduling, answering email, customer service, email campaigns, travel arrangements, social media. The list could go on and on depending on what type of VA you hire. I use Zirtual and am very happy with them. I have a dedicated VA for eight hours per month. At first I thought I would have trouble filling up eight hours but then I gave over my scheduling and the tasks that were 'nice to have' but not absolutes for my business. Those were tasks that repeatedly got pushed forward because they weren't a necessity but I wanted them to be done. Having her take over the scheduling was beautiful. She doesn't let me slide when someone is trying to infringe on my GSD Days and she keeps my meetings shorter so I can be more productive. If you go with Zirtual, tell them you read about it in my book! If you want VIP service, shoot me an email and I'll get you on the fast track ☺

There are also plans like Fancy Hands that you pay by task instead of by hour. You don't get a dedicated VA this way but paying by task can sometimes work in your favor. Don't have time to be on hold for 20 minutes with tech support? Fancy Hands will hold for you and patch you in when they join. Need some research for your summer vacay? Fancy Hands can research it for you.

Procrastinate creatively. Give a VA all those tasks you don't like doing but they need to get done. Spend your time in your line of genius.

Not sure how to calculate how much your time is worth? How much do you want to make this year or how much do you make per hour? Divide by 12. Divide that by 52 weeks per year. Divide again by # of hours you want to work per day = Bingo. This is how much your time is worth. If you're worth $96 per hour than hiring a VA for $30 per hour for 8 hours a month will let you focus your time on what matters most.

Step 5 – Parties, Conferences, Meetings

The Business Breakfast Meeting

This can be one of the hardest meetings because you either have too many options or too few. Business meetings or conferences tend to feed you into a coma. It starts out with breakfast, typically consisting of sugar-laden, refined carbohydrates like bagels, donuts and muffins. These bagels and muffins are 2-4 sizes of a true serving. If you are lucky they may have fruit and hard-boiled eggs. If these are your options, stick with those or if they have unsweetened yogurt, add some fruit. That's a long shot though as it is really hard to find unsweetened yogurt outside of a grocery store. I always take a small bag of nuts or eat something in my room *before* the breakfast meeting just in case they won't have anything healthy to eat. If you know you are going to eat something no matter what and you must have a bagel or muffin, eat only half and try to balance it with some healthy fat or protein like nut butter or a small dollop of cream cheese.

Coffee, tea, soda and juice are typically served all day long. Be careful with drinking your calories and caffeinating yourself to death. If you know you will drink coffee all day, try to make every other cup decaf coffee, decaf tea or water. Drinking tea or water all day will keep your hands busy and possibly keep you from mindless eating. To cut back on calories from juice, dilute it with some water. It will last longer, you won't get as much of a rush from the fruit sugar and if you drink less of it, you have saved yourself some much needed calories for the business lunch.

The Business Lunch

If the business lunch is served buffet style, you may have so many options you overdo it. Alternatively, if you have several food rules, you may end up eating one thing. Who among the vegetarians has survived on nothing but salad or bread for days during business conferences? When I first became a vegetarian at 19 and there wasn't anything for me to eat, I skipped the meat and ate twice the dessert or bread. Sometimes you have to ask yourself if your food rules need to be flexible in order to eat a *healthier* option. What are food rules? What you will or won't eat or in what way. For example, I don't eat pork, ever but after needing to change my diet due to Hashimoto's Disease, I now eat beef if it's grass-fed, chicken if it's antibiotic and hormone free, wild game and wild fish. I eat sweets only on the weekends and I eat very few fried foods, especially at restaurants. Restaurants are typically only required to change their oil out once a week so instead of risking getting food cooked in rancid oil, I opt not to have anything fried. Ask the restaurant before you order what day they changed their oil. It might help you make a decision. I try to avoid natural flavors, artificial sweeteners and cellulose because I don't think eating wood is good for anyone.

Did you know that natural flavors could be anything found in nature, including castoreum, which are anal secretions from a beaver's butt? This might be used in strawberry oatmeal instead of actual strawberries. Vote with your dollars and avoid beaver butt! FDA 21CFR101.22

If you are choosing to eat a certain way for ethical reasons, for example, you are vegetarian or vegan because you don't believe in the mistreatment or death of animals, you may not be as flexible, however if you are vegetarian for your health and the options are eat nothing all day or eat soup made with chicken broth, you may question which is the healthier option for you. Even though sometimes it is easier at a restaurant or when I am with people to say I am vegetarian, in truth, I eat a *mostly* plant-based diet and assume that most restaurant meat isn't going to meet my food rules.

If your lunch or dinner is buffet style, I recommend fixing a big salad first, paying careful attention to the amount of cheese and croutons you add to it. Place your dressing on the side and dip your fork in the dressing BEFORE picking up your food with it. I actually prefer just using vinegar and oil or just straight balsamic vinegar since most prepared dressings are full of sugar, sodium and fillers.

Most people take a second trip to the buffet and if you know you will, having a salad, some raw veggies or a cup of soup *first* may help you make a smarter choice on the second round than if you just went through and started loading up your plate the first time without a conscious plan. You will be able to see what is there and consider where you want to focus your calories.

There was a study that showed that thinner people scope out the salad bar or buffet first and then go back and fix their plate. Overweight or obese people tended to just get in line without determining how much food was on the buffet or what they wanted to choose

Business Sugar Coma

A business meeting or meal doesn't usually exist without some kind of coma-inducing, calorie-infested, high-fat dessert. Now, if they have a cheesecake you really want, go for it, but you will have to cut back somewhere. I personally don't recommend having ANY sugar at lunchtime, because in meetings all you are doing is sitting there and you will crash in the afternoon. In my former company it was common to order heavy desserts or at least cookies and brownies at lunch. As a corporate trainer, I used to do that too and then switched to having a fruit salad for the afternoon break. I only ever had two people complain that I didn't offer sweets and the few times I did, I was able to point out how tired people were in the afternoon!

I will say that sometimes it is important to splurge. When I was in New Orleans for the first time I happened to be with a friend and colleague and had to try a beignet. I didn't know if I would ever be back, it was something special we shared together and that was something I couldn't get back home. Bonus that I was there on a Saturday so I still kept my food rule! I also had to eat Alfajores dulce de leche sandwich cookies every time I went to Argentina.

Business Meeting Time Out

At some point during an all day meeting, either during a break or at lunch, it is important that you excuse yourself and consider the opportunity to get in 5-10 minutes of movement. Doing this before lunch will guarantee that you will do it and probably eat less because you will have less time at the meal. You can do it after you eat but you risk eating more than you should and not giving yourself the time out.

What do you do during your time out? Go to your hotel room, office, outside or even the bathroom and do a quick 5-minute stretching routine and some exercises that won't make you sweat. It will make you feel better and more energized, get your heart rate up a little bit or slow it down if it is a particularly heated meeting, and keep you from continuing to eat from the buffet. No one has to know you are doing this since many people pop back to their room or otherwise excuse themselves for some privacy. If you can, taking a walk outside is even better and you may be able to find someone to go with you.

The Business Dinner

How many people have been in a situation where there are 8-10 people and they insist on ordering five appetizers, everyone orders a meal and then someone orders a round of desserts for the table? Tell yourself you will just take small bites of the things you REALLY like and you wouldn't get at home. It isn't realistic for most people to say they will be able to refuse when several plates are being passed around. Instead, just think 'what are my favorite things here?' If you only think egg rolls are 'okay' but you would trade your iPhone for some crispy green beans, have a few crispy green beans and pass on the egg rolls. This way the attention isn't drawn to you if you don't want it to be and you are still enjoying your meal and socializing.

Restaurant Bombs

There are many restaurants where you can get good quality food, however many times the issue is *quantity* of food. Restaurants serve way too much. Most people would never eat as much at home as they do in a restaurant. It is also part of our culture not to waste food. How many people have eaten past being satisfied because they couldn't take what's left back to their hotel and they felt bad about not finishing it? Guess what? The meal costs the same whether it ends up in the trash, on your butt or your belly. And if you are traveling for business, your meal is reimbursable or deductible so leave it. Personally, I think that a lot of restaurants serve *quantity* when they can't serve *quality*.

Let's look at some examples, keeping in mind the average recommended calorie intake of 1800-2200 calories a day and less than 1500mg of sodium:

- Cheesecake Factory pasta carbonara w/ chicken has 2500 calories and 1630mg of sodium. More than an entire day's worth of sodium! I was pleased last summer to find a new menu called Skinnylicious at the Cheesecake Factory that actually had very tasty and reasonably sized options! I tried the veggie burger and it was yummo.

- PF Chang's chicken lo mein has 2050 mg of sodium, 1240 calories and 25 grams of fat.

- Applebee's pecan crusted chicken salad is a nutritional nightmare at 1360 calories and 80 – a whopping 80 grams of fat!!! It also has 2640 mg of sodium, which will make you swell up and bloat until you need to buy a new pair of elastic waist pants.

- A Smoothie King Cranberry Supreme has 1108 calories and 192 grams of sugar. Considering a daily limit of sugar is about 30 grams, this is over 6 times what you should have in one day. You just drank almost a week's worth of sugar. Was it worth it?

- Lastly, we have the Ruby Tuesday avocado turkey burger. Think you are getting healthy because it is a turkey burger? This artery monstrosity has 1313 calories, 73 grams of fat and 3221 grams of sodium. You just ate two days worth of sodium. Still want fries with that?

One website and book I like is Eat This, Not That. Men's Health put this out a few years ago and gives the better choices at restaurants. I applaud their work.

Fast Casual

Some easy places to eat healthy that is also is inexpensive and fast are fast casual restaurants like Moe's Southwest, where they have tofu if you are a vegetarian, or Chipotle. Chipotle was named one of the best gluten-free friendly restaurants. These places you can get a nice burrito bowl and load up on the veggies and ask for half or no cheese and sour cream. Panera Bread, Atlanta Bread Company and Jason's Deli have healthy soups and salads if you don't load up on the dressings. I love restaurants like Panera or Atlanta Bread, where you can get half sizes or 'you pick two'. Au Bon Pain has 'small plates' and a kiosk so you can look up nutritional information before you order. Jason's Deli and Atlanta Bread Company has several organic items. Noodles & Company has lean, hormone and antibiotic free meats and organic tofu. Zoe's Kitchen has several healthy items that are fresh with reasonable portions. All of these have several gluten-free and Paleo options.

Breakfast Bombs

We've already discussed the calories in a muffin or scone, which can be about 450. Would you eat a cupcake for breakfast?

Muffins are cupcakes without icing. There are definitely ways to make muffins healthy but I bet the ones you are buying aren't trying to go that route.

Beware of items like Dunkin Donuts egg white veggie flatbread. I used to eat these only to find out that besides their being highly processed and have over 30% of the daily max for sodium; they contain azodicarbonamide as a dough conditioner. This is banned in Europe due to studies showing it can cause asthma or allergic reactions. A Subway egg white flatbread isn't quite as bad but is very high in sodium. A McDonald's egg white delight or egg McMuffin, which somehow always ends up on a 'not so bad to eat list' has trans-fats, over 30% of your daily max for sodium, and nitrites and nitrates. When nitrates and nitrites are broken down in the stomach they have been shown to cause cancer in young children and pregnant women.

The use of azodicarbonamide in food carries a hefty fine up to $450,000 or 15-year jail sentence in Singapore.

For these types of fast food breakfasts, I like Einstein Bagel's egg white and asparagus sandwich. Bruegger's also has a skinny bagel sandwich with egg whites. These would be the better choices.

If eating in the hotel, try hard boiled-eggs, veggie omelets, whole grain toast, cottage cheese, fruit, and oatmeal. Steer clear of the pancakes and waffles. The sugar crash will bring you down quickly and again, it is basically like eating cake and icing for breakfast. These should really just be eaten as treats, not something to start your day with when you need energy.

The Forgotten Choice

People forget about grocery stores when they travel. If you are staying at an extended stay or a hotel with a mini kitchen it's super easy to eat healthy on the road. Even if you don't have a kitchen, many hotels come with a mini fridge or microwave (or you can ask for one in your room). I ate all of my dinners from a Publix grocery store for three nights in a row when traveling last year. I would get a big prepared fruit salad, edamame, grape tomatoes, a salad, hummus and nuts. None of these needed to be prepared or heated. If you eat meat, it is easy to get a grilled chicken breast or salmon. If you are lucky enough to be near a Whole Foods, Earth Fare or Trader Joe's, you will be in luck getting organic, prepared food from their deli/restaurant areas. I would eat these over most restaurant choices any day!

Apps

How does a person figure all of these things out? Apps! These are my most frequently used pocket friends:

- *Fooducate* gives food a grade from A – F and rates them according to their food category. That way, if you are really craving a muffin it will at least tell you which is the 'least bad' muffin to eat. They also have a premium service for gluten-free and diabetes. I have the gluten-free and I can quickly see if an item is GF by the green asterisk beside the item. It has scanning capability so I don't even have to enter it by hand.

- *My Fitness Pal* has an enormous food database that includes many restaurants. It is a nutrient and exercise tracker. *Lose It is a similar app.*

- Environmental Working Group *Dirty Dozen*, which tells you the fruits and vegetables you need to choose organic because they are the highest in pesticides

- *Find Me Gluten Free* helps you find gluten free restaurants based on your area.

#1 Biggest Mistake

What is the #1 biggest mistake you can make as a mobile professional when it comes to food? Eating every meal like you are 'going out for dinner'. How many of you try to 'eat your per diem'? If you get $75.00 per day, you feel like you have to spend it. You have only spent $30.00 today on food so you end up ordering a couple of drinks, an appetizer and a dessert with your dinner. When you are eating three meals a day plus snacks on someone else's dime, you *can't see every meal as a treat*. I used to treat myself with a Frappuccino every day when I traveled. Then I switched to Frappuccino Light. Later I realized that because I was traveling 2-4 days per week, I was taking in an enormous amount of sugar and that Frappuccino was really a dessert I was drinking at 10:00am! It was no longer a treat because I was doing it almost every day.

On the flip side, I have seen people almost starve themselves or eat very low quality food because they get to keep what they don't spend. When I had a job like this I ended up paying a lot more attention to what I bought, however I ended up going to grocery stores more so I could save my money and spend it on other things.

Questions to ask yourself when eating on per diem are:

1. Would I buy this much food if I were paying for it myself?

2. Am I buying this food because I'm hungry or because I feel like I'm burning a hole in my pocket?

When you travel frequently for business, you are **not** on vacation and it is **not** a treat. Eat like you would eat at home.

This book isn't a book on nutrition or a specific diet plan because there are many different appropriate and good plans, but I will state some of the more common mistakes among business travelers besides eating every meal like you are out for dinner.

1) Eating too much sugar. I don't think I need to go in to too much detail here but sugar is inflammatory, creates energy highs and lows, is empty calories and nutritionally devoid of benefits.

2) Eating too many processed foods. Convenience tends to win out for a majority of mobile pros but ask yourself if you are committed to being healthier and committed to having more energy. If you are committed, you'll be able to find a way with the tips I've shared, at least 75% of the time.

3) Not eating enough vegetables. Get them in when you can. Remember that your meal in the airport may not have any vegetables so if you have to load up earlier in the day, then do so. Your *meals* may not all be balanced but over the course of the day your *nutrition* can be.

4) Caffeinating to death. Discussed above and much like sugar, creates energy highs and lows. Use in a way that is smart. If you know you will need it or want it, wait until you actually do need it and if you drink a lot of it, try alternating with tea. That is what I do and I find it is helpful. For me, it's more the hot beverage in my hand and the comfort of it than the actual caffeine unless I'm changing time zones. I now get my fix with Teeccino coffee alternative. It's a very healthy herbal coffee that still has the dark feel of coffee.

I called my niece Ava Grace after her second day of First Grade and asked her how she liked it.

"It's hard." – Ava

"Oh no! What's hard about it?" – Me

"All of it. You know Aunt Marcey, I just want to eat and play. That's all I want to do". - Ava

"Well, Ava, I can't really argue with that". – Me

Step 6 – Home

Being a mobile professional doesn't just require health and productivity on the road. In order to be at your most awesome you also need to have a system at home as well. Every mobile pro knows that being gone for 3-4 days means catching up at home on the weekend. We want to eliminate as much of that catch-up feeling as possible and be able to relax or do what you need to do now.

Relationships and Connection

Maintaining your relationships at home and the ability to connect via text, phone or email with friends and family has major affects on business travelers and according to CLT, more so for women. It is much easier to stay connected now than a decade ago. Now we have Skype, Google Hangout or Facetime, can email or text easily and can share photos and videos for free. Being able to maintain some type of contact is important for your stress level, especially if you have kids.

If you are a very frequent business traveler, it is important to prioritize activities to ensure that your relationship doesn't suffer. When I first started traveling, about five years into our marriage in 1998, it was fun and exciting for both of us. My husband could stay up late, play his drums, order pizza and hang out with friends whenever I was gone. It felt like he was a bachelor again and it was a little fun for him. I could walk around new cities, hang out in hotels and not have to consider housework or chores. On the weekends when I was home we would do things together and it made the time we were together more special. Fast-forward a year and the remodeling of a house. My husband spent all week working on our house and I spent all week traveling. On the weekends all I wanted to do was work on the house and eat simple meals at home because I was sick of restaurant food. My husband just wanted to get OUT of the house and eat at a restaurant. After a few years we got into a routine. There were ups and downs with traveling but there are a few things I made sure I started doing along the way and some tips I've learned from others that you should definitely try.

- Have a weekly date. My husband and I have had a date, just the two of us, every week since October 1993 except for when I was gone for more than a week. This is sacred and when we have been really busy and I was gone for part of the week and then we had people staying with us on the weekend, we would at least sneak out for a coffee or something to make sure we had alone time.

- Leave notes. Sometimes I'll leave little love notes or stickies around the house, hiding in a place I know he will go, like the cereal box. It doesn't matter how old you are, finding a sticky with 'Have a great day!' will make you ☺

- Do something before you leave that will make their life easier. I tend to use Sundays as prep and cook time for the week. I cut vegetables, cook entrees and sides and if I am going to be gone, I make sure it is something my husband will find *very* easy to fix. He doesn't always eat what I leave behind but at least he knows that I thought of him while I was gone. If you don't cook, think of some other household task that you could do or something that can be done remotely like pay bills, schedule appointments, interview contractors etc.

- Share your riches. I used to bring home sweets and treats when I was a sugar addict, then I started buying healthier snacks in airports like bags of nuts or a fruit salad on my way out of the airport to take home to my husband to take to work the next day. When I was paid a set amount per day instead of reimbursed for my receipts, I loaded $10.00 on his Starbucks card every time he took me to the airport. I preferred it to parking in the garage and he got free Starbucks!

- Watch a show together. One of the best decisions I have made in my adult life (and I'm not kidding) is getting rid of cable and television. Not only is it expensive, but it is a huge Timesuck. Instead, we have Netflix. For less than $9 per month, we can stream to our TV and computer and watch whenever we want with NO commercials! If you have a show you like to watch together, you can both watch at the same time. Most couples aren't talking constantly to each other when they are at home so calling each other after one day away may not result in a lot of conversation but watching your favorite show together gives a sense of togetherness.

- Check out the website http://www.everydaybetterliving.com/love_danger_signs/100_questions.html to get ideas for questions to ask your significant other on the phone. Not everyone has an exciting day but asking a new and thought-provoking question every call can be fun! My husband and I spent a year going through the book *If – Questions for the Game of Life* when we were on vacation or road trips. I highly recommend it for couples and close friends.

- Connect in different ways besides the phone. Skype, Facetime, texting and emailing all give variety. A handwritten or sent card in the mail is really thoughtful. I only did this once because my husband rarely gets the mail when I am gone so I ended up picking up my own letter!

- Use the time on the road wisely so you don't have to do it at home. If I have things I need to read or research, I try to do as much on the road so that I have more time when I'm at home.

- Take your significant other with you! I know a woman who owns her own business and is able to do some of the work remotely. She travels often with her husband when he is traveling by car. They get to have a nice dinner and she can sometimes take in the sites of the city she is in. I have only taken my husband with me a couple of times but my brother has gone to Tokyo, Beijing and Miami with me for a very cheap vacation. It was fun to have him with me, made it safer to tour around and he got a free hotel! I also ate really cheap so he got most of his meals within my per diem.

Every relationship is tough but having one partner a business traveler means more conscious effort. Trust and empathy is key. The partner at home needs to understand how tiring the travel may be and that it isn't always nice restaurants and cush hotel accommodations. Often it is sub-par food, being 'on' at meetings all day and dealing with flight delays. The traveler needs to understand that the partner at home has to deal with all the home chores, especially if they have kids, alone without support. Routines and schedules may become more important when one person travels. The extra steps are worth it for your relationship and your sanity.

Physical Productivity

Do you ever feel like you take too much stuff with you on your trips but yet you never have what you need? Do you feel like your house falls apart the moment you step out the door? Do you spend too much time searching your bag or your luggage trying to find what you need?

Having less stuff in general is helpful as far as clutter and decision-making. When I drastically reduced my wardrobe it actually made it easier for me to pack and get dressed because I didn't have as many choices to make. I also made sure that every time I bought something, it already went with something I had or could serve more than one purpose.

Making Your Home Easier for Travel

Traveling for business requires organization and planning if you don't want your house to fall apart. Common issues include: mail doesn't get picked up, bills don't get paid, the house doesn't get cleaned, clothes don't get washed, groceries don't get bought, appointments don't get scheduled or have to be cancelled at the last minute. When I used to travel weekly, I felt like all I did on the weekend was catch up on my life tasks before it started all over again. Not all of the recommendations will work for everyone, but these are what worked for me.

Mail

I have any bill that I can delivered electronically either to my bank or to my inbox so I never miss a payment. Some of them are on auto-pay so I don't even have to worry about the actual payment. This may seem like a no-brainer but I'm always surprised how many people still have a paper bill sent to them. With File This Fetch, I always have the statement available, organized within my Google Drive. If I'm going to be gone more than a week, I put a hold on my mail. For safety reasons, you should have your newspaper (if you still get them) stopped. An easy target for thieves is a home with a few newspapers out front. It is obvious you aren't home.

As mentioned before, I highly recommend SendOut cards for marketing, birthdays, anniversaries and holidays. I am able to send cards from anywhere – office, airport, hotel, or coffee shop and can schedule them in advance. Easy peasy.

Paper Junk Mail

Need to get rid of paper clutter and junk mail? I have eliminated most of my unwanted mail and am able to go to the mailbox some days and not have any mail. Lovely.

DMAChoice.org (Direct Marketing Association) is a free mail preference service where you can opt out of junk mail via email. If you don't want any catalogs, magazine offers or credit card offers, you can opt out of that category entirely. It saves you from having to recycle and from seeing something you have to buy to keep up with Mr. and Mrs. Jones. Unfortunately, there is no opt-out for political ads. Grrrr…. You can also register on DMAChoice for the deceased or as a caretaker.

CatalogChoice.org is complementary to DMAChoice. I use it for opting out of specific magazines and catalogs. A great feature is the ability to opt-down instead of opt-out. If you want Victoria's Secret quarterly instead of weekly, the site has the capability to do that for companies that will allow it. As of October 2013, I had saved three fully-grown trees, 920 pounds of greenhouse gas, 326 pounds of solid waste and 2215 gallons of water by opting out!

OptOutPreScreen.com will allow you to opt out of credit cards for five years or permanently. I only have one credit card and it is the same one I have had for 15 years so I opted out years ago. Unfortunately, I was still getting credit card offers sent to my business account so I put a freeze on all credit card offers. This helps protect me from identity theft because a credit card can't be opened in my name without my unfreezing the account. It only takes a few days to thaw it if I really needed a new credit card but since I have only ever needed one, I don't see that needing to happen. It is definitely worth the peace of mind for me to just have it frozen.

Paper Karma is an app for your phone. Simply snap a photo of the envelope with the Sender and Recipient in focus and they will contact the mailer to have you removed from the distribution list. I love this app and snap my photos right over the recycle bin before the mail ever goes in my house!

House Cleaning

When I'm traveling heavily, I enlist the services of a housecleaner/marriage saver twice a month. I like my house clean and my cleanliness standards are different from my husband, so in order for me to keep from spending the time I have at home on cleaning my house or nagging my husband, I just suck it up and pay someone. When I'm not traveling, we have figured out a system that works pretty well for us. I divided our house into zones and every Sunday when we have our family meeting, we choose which zones we want to do. He works outside the home six days a week and I work from my home office when I'm not working with clients. I take on most of the zones if I have a home-based week and he takes on less. I made a list of tasks for each zone so whatever zone he is cleaning he knows the different tasks that need to be done. This can also be great for families with kids or if you have roommates.

It's funny how many times people have come in to my home and remarked how clean it is. I always tell them it isn't that my house is so clean, but more that I don't have a lot of clutter, which gives the illusion of cleanliness. However, the less stuff to move around, pick up, sweep around and put away, the faster any cleaning routine will be!

I timecap my housecleaning too. I set the timer for 25 minutes every day and do as much as I can until I hear that beep of freedom. If it didn't get done then it's not going to. Life's too short.

Wardrobe

I don't have a lot of clothes, especially business clothes, so I need to do laundry in between all of my trips. I put my clothes directly into the washer straight from my suitcase. Waiting any longer also puts my workout clothes at risk for mildew so I don't let them sit too long. After I wash and dry, the clothes go right back into the suitcase if I'm going on another trip. I also try to avoid clothes that are dry-clean only because it is another errand I have to run, is costly, and most dry cleaning is harmful to the environment.

I've already spoken about having clothes to mix and match, that don't wrinkle and you actually wear. Save yourself the space in your closet, time and energy deciding what to wear and money buying items that won't go with anything else or holding on to items that you could consign or sell.

Sometimes I save clothes as 'throw-away clothes' when I'm going on vacation or somewhere that I know I will be shopping. Clothes that I plan to donate because I no longer want them, not because they are stained, torn or ill fitting, get saved as throwaway clothes. This way as I wear them I can toss them or neatly fold them and leave them for housekeeping or lost and found for someone to take. I had a few sweaters that were too big for me and instead of taking them to Goodwill, I neatly folded them and left them on the bed with a note that said 'I no longer want these. Please distribute to someone in need'. Housekeepers don't make a lot of money. If they don't want them they can give them to someone else or if they don't want the hassle they can throw them away.

Community Supported Agriculture (CSA)

I belong to a Community Supported Agriculture program that I have referred at least 12 people to. If they had a cheerleader program, I would sign up - 'Go Papa Spuds!'. While I can't believe any CSAs are as good as my *Papa Spuds*, I'm sure there are wonderful ones all over and I highly recommend joining one. The benefits go beyond having produce delivered to your door. You are supporting local and small farms, many of which are pesticide-free or organic and you learn to eat what is in season and how to experiment. We can get our veggies, fruits, cheese, bread, meat, spices, sauces, mushrooms, eggs and coffee from our CSA. It is super convenient because I can go online every Friday and choose what I want to order and it gets delivered straight to my door on Wednesdays!

While I am a huge proponent of CSAs, I also understand if people are traveling and there isn't anyone to pick up their box (not all CSAs deliver) or take it inside their home to refrigerate it, that this might not be a good idea. There is also an issue with time. I admit; cleaning, peeling, chopping and prepping vegetables takes a lot of time and if time is of the essence, buy it ready to fix. Pre-washed salads and pre-washed and chopped vegetables and fruit will help you to eat healthier. I always buy giant bags of frozen organic berries at the wholesale club so I have them on hand for breakfast and smoothies. When it comes to veggies and fruits, buy them however you will eat it but please try not to buy it loaded with salt or sugar.

Food Prep

Sundays tend to be my days to make food for the week. I set the timer for one hour and do as much as I can during that time. I wash and prep veggies and fruit, cook some kind of grain like rice, buckwheat or quinoa, throw some dried beans in the crockpot that I had soaked overnight and sauté or grill hormone and antibiotic-free, no crap added meat. I also make baggies of muesli mix for my husband for the week. This has become a favorite of his daily meal plan and while it takes a bit of time it is worth it because he eats a healthy breakfast. I use to make it for myself but after needing to go gluten-free due to Hashimoto's Disease, I opt out.

Muesli Mix includes:

40grams Bob's Red Mill gluten-free muesli

.5 Tablespoons of chia seeds and/or 1 Tablespoon of flax meal

.5 ounce of nuts

.5 scoop Vega Sports Performance Protein Powder

Every night I put a baggie of muesli mix in a bowl with .75 cup of frozen organic berries or other fruit and 4-5 ounces of unsweetened almond or coconut milk and stick it in the fridge. By the morning the fruit has thawed, the muesli has thickened up and it is delicious and easy! The muesli mix is great to travel with to add to yogurt or milk and fruit at a hotel.

Action!

Now we are at the end of the guide to being healthy and productive on the road. I have shared hacks that you can incorporate into your daily life. Some will work for you and others won't. Some you will try and others you will dismiss immediately. If you are the type of person that lets life happen **to** you instead of being in control of it then you wasted your money buying this book.

Ask yourself who you want to be: A mobile professional who is tired, unhealthy, lacks energy, has 1000 emails in their inbox, is drowning in tasks, always forgets to pack something to eat, is unable to catch up when they are home and puts themselves at a safety risk when on the road…

Or

A mobile professional who is healthy, physically fit, rarely gets sick, is confident about himself or herself, has control over their calendar and inbox, has streamlined their packing, can enjoy the time they are home, and is alert and aware, allowing themselves to balance work and play?

Which of these are you *now* and which do you want to *be*? Which of these mobile professionals do you think would say they *Work Well* so they can *Play More*?

I imagine you want to be the second mobile professional, so now I refer back to the beginning of the book. Ask yourself the following:

1. What are your goals?

   a. Who do you want to be?

   b. How do you want it to look?

   c. What do you want to feel?

2. What's your whine?

   a. What is your excuse?

   b. Who or what is standing in your way (or who/what do you *perceive* is standing in your way?)

3. What's your win?

   a. What kind of resources do you have?

   b. Who can help you or hold you accountable?

4. What's your plan?

   a. SMART goals: Specific, Measureable, Attainable, Realistic and Timely

A goal without a plan is just a dream.

Consider the different categories, chapters and topics and determine ONE thing that you can change now. The first behavior change should be easy. Give yourself a timeline that is realistic. If it is something that you won't have trouble with, maybe it is a week. If it might take some time, try 4-6 weeks. Use an app like Lift.do to track your behavior change. If you are really ambitious try one thing in each category, but don't try any more than that in the beginning.

If you need coaching in behavior change, please contact me to help guide you in the right direction. I can give you a realistic customized plan, provide accountability and put you on the path to achieving your goals. You can be a productive and healthy mobile professional! I would love to be part of your journey. Please share your habit changes via Facebook at MarceyRaderCoaching, send me a tweet to @MarceyRader or contact me through my website www.marceyrader.com.

Work Well and Play More!

Author Bio

Marcey Rader is a Lifestyle Trainer with a B.S in Exercise Science, M.Ed. in Health Promotion, is certified by the National Academy of Sports Medicine as a Certified Personal Trainer and is a Certified Productive Environment Specialist. She is the creator of the **Jetsetter Exercise Kit** (www.jetsettergymkit.com), and the **25 in 25**® and **10 by 10**® exercise challenges with Lift.do. She provides customized health and productivity solutions to mobile professionals, works with small businesses and is a professional speaker. Her primary goal in life is to Work Well, Play More and feel like a superhero. Don't you want to?

Made in the USA
Middletown, DE
04 November 2017